THE BIG PIVOT

**Shifting Your Leadership Focus
from Outward Success to Inward Growth**

Mike Moore

The BIG Pivot:
Shifting Your Leadership Focus from Outward Success to Inward Growth

Copyright © 2025 by Mike Moore

Published in the United States by Mike Moore Ministries, Inc.

www.mikemoore.com

Hardback ISBN 978-1-7369777-4-3| eBook ISBN 978-1-7369777-6-7 |
Audiobook ISBN: 978-1-7369777-5-0

Printed in the United States of America

All rights reserved. No part of this book may be reproduced, stored in a retrieval system, or transmitted in any form or by any means without expressed written permission of the author.

Any internet addresses (websites, blogs, etc.) in this book are offered as a resource. They are not intended in any way to be or imply an endorsement by Mike Moore Ministries, nor does Mike Moore Ministries vouch for the content of these sites for the life of this book.

Unless otherwise indicated, all Scripture quotations are taken from the New *King James Versio*n, © 1979, 1980, 1982, 1984 by Thomas Nelson, Inc. Used by permission. All rights reserved.

Scriptures marked KJV are taken from the KING JAMES VERSION (KJV): KING JAMES VERSION, public domain.

Scriptures marked (NLT) are taken from the Holy Bible, New Living Translation, copyright © 1996, 2004, 2007, 2013, 2015 by Tyndale House Foundation. Used by permission of Tyndale House Publishers Inc., Carol Stream, Illinois 60188. All rights reserved.

Scripture marked (NIV) taken from THE HOLY BIBLE, NEW INTERNATIONAL VERSION®, NIV® Copyright © 1973, 1978, 1984, 2011 by Biblica, Inc.® Used by permission. All rights reserved worldwide.

Scripture quotations marked (TLB) are taken from The Living Bible, copyright © 1971 by Tyndale House Foundation. Used by permission of Tyndale House Publishers, Carol Stream, Illinois 60188. All rights reserved.

All Scripture marked with the designation (GW) is taken from GOD'S WORD®. © 1995, 2003, 2013, 2014, 2019, 2020 by God's Word to the Nations Mission Society. Used by permission.

Scriptures taken from The Message (MSG). Copyright © 1993, 1994, 1995, 1996, 2000, 2001, 2002. Used by permission of NavPress Publishing Group.

Scripture quotations taken from the Amplified® Bible (AMP), Copyright © 2015 by The Lockman Foundation. Used by permission.

Scriptures taken from the Amplified® Bible, Classic Edition (AMPC). Copyright © 1954, 1958, 1962, 1964, 1965, 1987 by The Lockman Foundation. Used by permission.

*This book is dedicated to
the leaders and members of Faith Chapel
who allowed me to pastor you for over 40 years.
It was an honor to walk alongside you.
You were and still are the best church in the entire world.*

CONTENTS

	Dedication	iii
	Preface: My Story	vii
	Introduction	ix
1.	Leadership Is	1

TRAIT ONE:
PIVOT FROM A BIG REPUTATION TO GOOD CHARACTER

2.	Good Character Is Spiritual	11
3.	Integrity	17
4.	Faithfulness	35
5.	Stewardship	41

TRAIT TWO:
PIVOT FROM BIG STARTS TO DISCIPLINE

6.	You Must Be Disciplined	51
7.	You Must Commit	57
8.	You Must Focus	71
9.	You Must Finish	79

TRAIT THREE:
PIVOT FROM BIG SHOT TO HUMILITY

10. Prideful Leadership … 85

11. Listen to Others … 93

TRAIT FOUR:
PIVOT FROM BIG WIMP TO COURAGE

12. Be Brave, Conquer Fear … 101

13. Courage to Lead … 111

TRAIT FIVE:
PIVOT FROM BIG TALK TO COMPETENCE

14. Talk Less, Grow More … 117

15. Knowledge and Skills … 125

Conclusion … 133

Notes … 135

About the Author … 139

About Mike Moore Ministries … 141

Resources … 143

PREFACE

My Story

Many decades ago, God chose me to lead in a way I never imagined—me, of all people. Basketball was everything to me. Thoughts of being drafted into the NBA consumed me, just like many young boys. Professional basketball was at the forefront of everything I did, but like most, I didn't make it. I did well academically and graduated from college but struggled to find a job. I was so focused on my "hoop dream" of making it to the NBA. When that burst, I realized I hadn't mentally prepared myself for anything else. I felt like a failure. Now what?

I shifted and decided to go to law school. I started feeling better about myself. You see, I grew up watching the fictional character Perry Mason who was a legal defense attorney. He was eloquent in the courtroom, smart, a great leader, yet fair. At the end of each episode, Perry Mason was considered a hero because he fought for justice for his wrongly accused clients. He always won. My new dream was to become a Black Perry Mason, but the Lord had other plans for me. After my first semester of law school in 1978, a Scripture in the book of Ezekiel visually jumped off the page, and I knew the Lord was calling me into full-time ministry. Initially, I was stunned. Then came disappointment because I convinced myself that if I was like Perry Mason, people would look up to me. I could speak on behalf of others, my wife and I wouldn't struggle financially, and I could be a BIG SHOT. This felt like yet another dream crushed, but I knew what God told me. So, I shifted again and obeyed Him.

I started learning all I could about ministry and His Word. I asked the Holy Spirit to teach me and began observing and studying other ministers from afar. Was I scared? Absolutely. Were there tough times? Most definitely, but I followed what God told me each step of the way. As I grew, I eventually prayed for Him to "burn the big shot out of me." The Lord led me into new territories as I pastored what others would consider a successful church for over 40 years.

I've come a long way since those early days. I have made mistakes and learned from them. Now, I believe I have a wealth of knowledge and experience to share with others. And I know God has been so faithful to me. And now that I've shifted from a senior pastor role, I know He has called me to coach and mentor leaders. I want to pour myself into leaders. And this is why I'm writing this book.

~ *Mike Moore*

"A man's mind plans his way [as he journeys through life], But the Lord directs his steps and establishes them."
(PROVERBS 16:9 AMP)

INTRODUCTION

The truth about today's world is that leadership is in short supply across all realms of society. No matter where you look—in business, government, family, education, healthcare, church, the military, or the community—the absence is clear and has far-reaching effects. The lack of true leadership has led to an environment where the pursuit of outward success and personas frequently takes precedence over everything else.

Business owners, CEOs of corporations, and influencers prioritize profits and their public image over the well-being of their employees, clients, and customers. Managers and volunteer team leaders have titles, but they are not leaders. The allure of power in government leads many elected officials astray from their duty to serve people. Even at home, trying to hide our vulnerabilities can create barriers in our relationships. Schools often emphasize grades and achievements over instilling essential values and traits in our children. Churches have lost their way due to a lack of leadership. There is a great need for leadership.

People think leading is bossing others around when nothing could be further from the truth. Followers crave authenticity from their leaders, but it's hard to find. The question of authenticity, or rather, the lack of it, is rampant in the public domain. In the age of social media, people may concoct an online reality that is at odds with their actual circumstances to appear like they have it all together. Leaders may resort to exaggerating accomplishments, skills, or possessions to garner approval and admiration inadvertently compromising their integrity in the process. Think of those who purposely pose for a photo in front of a luxury car to leave a false impression or to receive social likes, but the fact is they don't own the car—it's a rental. However, building a BIG REPUTATION on falsehoods is like building a house on sand. It won't withstand the test of time.

Don't fall for the trap! *The BIG Pivot* delves into why you should resist a leadership style that employs BIG as the core feature used to motivate, impress, or influence others. Do you ask yourself questions like the following?

- How can I inspire others to collaborate with me so that we can reach the next level?
- How can I motivate people to follow me?
- How can I attract more clients or customers?
- How do I lead my children?

This book provides the answer to these questions through the leadership principles found in this Scripture.

INTRODUCTION

Take heed to yourself and to the doctrine.
*Continue in them, for in doing this **you will save**
both yourself and those who hear you.*
(1 Timothy 4:16)

The Apostle Paul is giving his mentee Timothy instructions. Timothy became a phenomenal leader in his own right. He tells Timothy to *take heed (to give serious attention) to yourself* and then the doctrine. Notice the order. Before you take heed to what you're saying, showing, teaching, or instructing others, you should tend to yourself first and continue in the doctrine. In doing this, you will save yourself (notice the order again) and those who hear you (your followers). Personal development comes before leading others. Leading yourself is step one in leading others successfully. It will always be the greatest challenge you have as a leader.

It's time to make the BIG pivot! In basketball, *pivot* means the player shifts their weight on one foot while keeping that foot grounded to change direction to protect the ball from defenders and shoot or pass quickly. Leading yourself means pivoting from focusing on how BIG you appear to others (outward success) to focusing on grounded, inward growth. Lead yourself first by embracing the inner traits of good character, discipline, humility, courage, and competence, and others will enthusiastically follow! That's where true success lies. It all starts with you!

CHAPTER 1
LEADERSHIP IS

I am so excited about this opportunity to take you on a leadership journey. Leadership development is not an event or a destination. I want to inspire and equip you on this journey. As you read this book, I want you to apply the concepts to your leadership arena—whether in business, school, government, the military, church, healthcare, the community, or even within your household.

Whether you're aspiring to become a leader, in a new leadership role, or an experienced leader, you must master leading yourself to achieve success and longevity in leading others. First, let's establish a foundation so we're all on the same page. What is a leader? What do I mean by leadership?

I define leadership as...

LEADERSHIP {def}**:**
› The art of inspiring people to do something with a focus on people while delivering good results.

Leadership is an art. I do not mean art in the sense of a finished product like a painting, ceramics, or music. *Art*, in this definition, is a skill acquired by experience, study, and observation. Because leadership is an acquired skill, this means you can attain it. Leadership is the art of <u>inspiring</u>, not telling, commanding, or demanding. *Inspire* means to excite, encourage, and fill with the urge. I was particularly fascinated by the Latin definition of *inspire*, which is, "to breathe life into." **A leader breathes life into people.**

I believe that God has given every person the desire to achieve, win, and be good at something. That inner flame is an aspiration to succeed that God placed in the heart of every person. Nobody wants to fail. People want to win in life. Leaders must approach people with an understanding that there's a flame inside of them. However, circumstances, dysfunctional environments, negative experiences, disappointments, or rejection cause that flame to fade. It's a low flame. Imagine a fire and blowing air over a flame that is barely there. Science tells us that blowing a constant, gentle stream of air over a low flame causes the flame to glow and grow. Remember, the word *inspire* means "to breathe life into." Inspiration brings life back into the flame. That's what leaders should do. Good leaders blow gently over the flame when people come to us with a low flicker, helping what's inside of them glow. Unfortunately, those who are merely managing instead of leading can sometimes blow the flame out by applying harsh demands and rigid control.

The difference between a manager and a leader is clear. Leaders inspire and energize their teams, while ineffective managers stifle motivation and extinguish potential.

Mouth-to-mouth resuscitation is another example of what it means to inspire. Although some experts say it shouldn't be used anymore, let's think about the definition "to breathe life." In this instance, a person is not breathing, and you give them mouth-to-mouth resuscitation. You pinch their nose, put your mouth on their mouth, and you blow air into their mouth and their lungs. They awaken and begin to breathe! Think about it.

That's what true leadership does. They inspire and breathe life into team members who perform poorly or are not motivated. Contrast this with a person who is strictly a manager. They assume there is no hope for them and operate like a coroner, declaring them legally dead and issuing a death certificate. They say, "Let's find somebody else to get this done. I don't have time to deal with this." We must have a paradigm shift. As leaders, we must give mouth-to-mouth resuscitation. That's what it means to inspire. It involves not blowing out the flame in people but causing the flickering flame in followers to glow.

Let me revisit my mention of leaders and managers. Contrary to popular belief, leadership is not management. Being a leader does not mean having an official title. You can live up to the definition of leadership without having a title. Let's dispel the myth about what a manager is and what a leader is. A leader can be a manager, but a manager is not necessarily a leader. Here's the difference.

LEADERSHIP IS ABOUT...

- The *who* versus the *what*
- People versus things (budgets, resources, time, accountability)
- Empowerment versus control
- Motivation versus instructions
- Creativity (creating and innovating) versus administration
- Risk versus maintenance
- Developing people while achieving results versus achieving results only
- Creating leaders versus creating managers
- Having a high retention rate versus a high turnover rate

Remember the first part of our leadership definition, "...inspiring **people** to do something with a **focus on people**..." Let's unpack the tenets above. Notice the second line says leadership is about people, but management is about things. People should always come first—before tasks and productivity. Focus on them, and they'll feel inspired to accomplish what needs to be done. Great leaders get results while focusing on the people. Managers do not inspire others. They simply get things done. Followers are only doing things for the manager because they are being made to do it, not because they want to, and certainly not because they are inspired. We need a paradigm shift because we've put "getting things done" before caring about the people and connecting with them. We put "the doing" and tasks in front of people. We've put the cart before the horse. A leader is supposed to **inspire people to do** something. You are trying to motivate people to do tasks who have no understanding of you, and you have no understanding of them or their hopes, dreams, and desires. In many cases, we don't care as long as they do what we need them to do for us when we need them to do it. No! That shouldn't be so.

As parents, we bark out orders like, "Make up your bed" and "Get good grades," but we fail to connect with our children. When was the last time you had a real conversation with your school-age kids or teenagers to discover who they are? They have hopes and dreams, too. Do you even know what they are? Are you truly leading them, or are you just managing all the household tasks?

As a leader in your respective area, are you just demanding, "Give me this report," "Do this," "Do that," or "Never mind, I'll find someone else to do it"? Have you wondered why your subordinates aren't keeping up? Or why aren't they motivated to do anything for you? Have you ever asked them if your demands are unreasonable or not? Do you care?

Whether you are leading in school, work, church, or in your home, do you have a project-first mindset and not a people-first mindset? In other words, do you only have an orientation toward action but not an orientation toward relationships? Is there evidence that supports this (in your actions, behaviors, or results)?

Many of you are trying to get people to act, but you have no relationship with the people because you're too busy doing. I have heard leaders say, "I wish I could spend time with the people, but I've got so many things I must do." This is wrong thinking. John 3:16 says, *"For God so loved the world that He gave His only begotten Son, that whoever believes in Him should not perish but have everlasting life."* The reference to the world is not about the Earth. God so loved people that He gave. Leadership is a people business. It didn't say, "God so loved projects or tasks." You should not be in leadership if you do not have time for people. Evaluate yourself.

Our leadership definition says, "**… with a focus on people.**" We are too focused on the project, goals, outcomes, and tasks and not enough on the people we are trying to reach. We're also not focused on the people helping us to reach the people we are trying to reach. That includes your employees, staff, and volunteers. We take them for granted. You need the workers to get things done, but they don't really matter to you. Just know they will pick up on that and they won't be motivated under your leadership. YOU MUST SHIFT!

In a nutshell, if you are going to be in leadership and be effective as a leader, you must focus on the people, and that means you must care about them! When you care, it liberates ideas, energy, and the capacity of others to deliver good results. How do you exhibit care so that your followers and those helping you reach your followers feel the care? I have a formula that is simple but may prove to be a challenge for some of you to execute.

CARE = NEED + LISTENING + SUPPORT

Review the formula above. Let's start with understanding what it means to care. Care involves understanding the person's **needs**. Every person, regardless of their race, ethnicity, education level, or religious affiliation, has five basic needs: spiritual, physical, mental/emotional, relational, and financial. How do you and I become aware of people's specific needs as leaders? The answer is **listening**, which is the key to awareness. Care also involves **support**. I can say that I care about my spouse or my children, but is there evidence of that care? Support is not just words or intent. Care is always manifested through support. Is there physical evidence of your care? If I were to ask those who follow you if you care about them, what would they say?

Identify your gap(s) so you can grow your leadership and get the outcomes you want as a result. I believe repetition is the key to learning. As a result, here's a recap of our leadership definition with what we've learned plugged into it.

Leadership is **the art** (a skill acquired by experience, study, and observation) **of inspiring** (breathing life into) **people** (followers, your children, employees, volunteers, congregants, clients, etc.) **to do something** (things, tasks, projects, objectives) **with a focus on people** (caring, connecting) **while delivering good results** (the win, outcome).

This book does not focus on "delivering good results" as much because most of us already know this. Most business books talk about results. It is well-established. Managers absolutely get things done, and that's why we need management! I'm emphasizing that leaders get things done in a way that's different from managers. I'm challenging you to be a leader!

Now that you have an overview of leadership, let's dive right into our main topics. To lead others, you must first lead yourself successfully. So, the first item on this list is becoming a person of character.

TRAIT ONE

PIVOT
FROM A BIG REPUTATION TO

GOOD CHARACTER

"The next move of God will be in the area of character."

MIKE MOORE

CHAPTER 2

GOOD CHARACTER IS SPIRITUAL

Consider a prominent member of your community who leads initiatives, advocates for worthy causes, and is a focus of positive attention. This leader has built a strong reputation as someone who always does the right thing and is respected by others. The public regards them as a role model, always truthful and dedicated. However, they find it difficult to keep up those admirable traits when they are alone. They may make private decisions that contradict what they say or do in public and may be inconsistent with how they treat others one-on-one. This showcases the idea of a BIG REPUTATION (the image you present to everyone and the impression others have of you). However, if your BIG REPUTATION does not match your character, those you lead will not voluntarily follow you, and this will impact your influence. If you truly want to motivate others, inspire them, and be the good person they think you are, you must pivot from having a BIG REPUTATION in name only to developing good character.

CHARACTER {def}:
› the sum of a person's positive and negative traits —moral, mental, and ethical—when measured against an accepted standard of right and wrong
› the group of qualities that make a person different from others

Your character is you. It's your life. It is the way you carry yourself and how you handle people. If you think about it, most moral or leadership failures are character-based. Every leader will make mistakes and find themselves in the position of facing moral or ethical dilemmas. However, the DNA of your character will be the deciding factor in determining how you respond to and resolve those dilemmas. Character has two facets: a spiritual side and a practical side. We'll start by examining the spiritual aspect.

THE FRUIT OF THE SPIRIT

The DNA of your character should reflect the character of Jesus Christ. His character traits or nature can be found in Galatians 5:22-23. These traits were placed in seed form in the human spirit of the Christian at the new birth.

We commonly refer to this passage of Scripture as the *fruit of the spirit*, which is the foundation of good character. This spiritual fruit grows in the hearts and lives of believers. It is the standard we should use when determining right and wrong within ourselves. This is not to say that we should try to do the Holy Spirit's job and attempt to regulate what everyone else believes and how they behave. This DNA test is about you. What standard do you use to measure your character?

The *fruit of the spirit* developed and manifested in the everyday experiences of the believer is what makes Christians different from those who are not saved. It is important to know what this fruit is before you can implement it into your life.

As you might identify a grape variety by familiar traits such as color, sweetness, skin thickness, aroma, and juiciness, the *fruit of the spirit* is distinguished by nine character traits that become recognizable to anyone who interacts with a believer who demonstrates them. These Christlike traits make you more appealing to others.

> "But the fruit of the Spirit is love, joy, peace, longsuffering, gentleness, goodness, faith, meekness, temperance: against such there is no law."[1]

9 CHARACTER TRAITS OF THE FRUIT OF THE SPIRIT (CHRIST'S CHARACTER)

1. Love
   - unselfish concern for others[2]

2. Joy
   - an inner rejoicing not dependent on circumstances[3]

3. **Peace**
   - undisturbed mind and heart in good times or bad times[4]

4. **Longsuffering**
   - long tempered; not easily upset or disturbed by the faults, weaknesses, failures, or ignorance of others

5. **Gentleness**
   - kindness - compassionate, warm, cordial, nice, friendly, empathetic, flexible, thoughtful, helpful

6. **Goodness**
   - demonstrations in good works or acts shown towards others with no ulterior motive

7. **Faith**
   - faithfulness - relations to God and men
   - The three components of faithfulness are trustworthiness, dependability, and perseverance.

8. **Meekness**
   - a mindset of being teachable and submission to authority[5]

9. **Temperance**
   - self-control - the strength to stand against excess (thoughts, words, desires, emotions, eating, work, relationships, spending habits, and more)

Many of the characteristics are intertwined. Did you notice that love encompasses all the rest? John 13:34-35 says, "A new commandment I give to you, that you love one another; as I have loved you, that you also love one another. By **this** all will know that you are My disciples, if you have love for one another." This means good character sets you apart from others. Our leadership definition mentioned "the art of inspiring…" Imagine what heights your leadership could rise to if you matured in the *fruit of the spirit* by becoming more like Christ. It would truly inspire others. People would start to listen to you!

KINDNESS AND SPIRITUAL MATURITY SELF-REFLECTION TEST

- How do you respect and deal with children?
- How do you reprove or correct those who have sinned, made mistakes, or failed?

ACTIONS TO TAKE

1. When you reviewed the attributes of spiritual character, did you notice areas you needed to work on? You are responsible for your growth. Make a list of the areas where you need to improve and act on it the next time an opportunity arises this week. You will have plenty of opportunities to practice!
    - Example: If you are quick to anger, practice being slow to anger by not lashing out.

- Example: If people have told you that you are unapproachable, make a conscious effort to smile more.

2. Building on my earlier mention of grapes, did you know a grape does not ripen further once it is cut from the vine? The same is true for the *fruit of the spirit*. To grow the seed in you, you must *abide* (to stay joined to; to remain in, keep in fellowship; to be present; to be continually aware) in Jesus Christ.[6] Set aside a few minutes each day this week to abide in Christ.

3. Pivot from being solely concerned with having a BIG REPUTATION to putting in the effort to have a spiritually developed character. You don't have to do it alone. Ask the Holy Spirit to help you grow.

   - Example: Instead of proclaiming to be a believer on social media, at church, or work by using "Christian catchphrases," evaluate yourself to see if you are actually loving, compassionate, and gentle to those you disagree with and those who do not look like you. Remember, fruit is produced from a seed and grows and matures to the point that it is visible to others.

CHAPTER 3

INTEGRITY

In the next several chapters, we will explore character-building blocks essential to forming a strong foundation that will help you become a better version of yourself and achieve your leadership goals.

A solid personal foundation of good character sets you up for success in any role you play. Although great leadership is not about perfection, great leaders operate from a position of excellence in character. Jumping into your role without doing the internal work is a recipe for disaster. Let's begin this discussion of integrity as the first essential character-building block.

WHAT IS INTEGRITY?

There is a lot to be said about being a good, honest person who has integrity and tells the truth. Integrity is much broader in scope than just telling the truth. Integrity undergirds a person's entire character and is lived across the spectrum of a person's life. For instance, have you ever had someone tell you the truth, but you knew they intended to hurt you or embarrass you? Consider a leader who tells the truth about a mistake he made in taking a certain approach to achieve a goal, but he blames his subordinates for his error. It is possible to convey facts while purposefully creating a false impression of a situation. One could weaponize the truth with malicious intent, but technically, they told the truth.

Let's define my use of the word integrity. I have three definitions.

INTEGRITY {def}:
› wholeness—when there is alignment of our values, thoughts, feelings, words, and actions
› what we do when no one is looking; doing the right things in the unsupervised areas of our lives
› when who you are and who you appear to be are the same

JUDAS EXAMPLE

Judas, one of Jesus' twelve disciples, held a leadership position of trust as the group's treasurer—managing the money bag. The Scriptures say Judas was a thief who took money out of the treasury for his personal use.

He abused his position by stealing. It's obvious that he didn't steal from the money bag when others were looking. Why? He didn't have integrity. Integrity is who you are when no one is looking. It is doing the right thing in the unsupervised areas of your life. Are you in a trusted position? Do you have access to resources (money or human resources)? Have you figured out a way to cheat the system while also pretending to be morally upright to others?

Judas' BIG REPUTATION was that he was a devoted follower of Christ, but in his private life, he was a thief. Wholeness is when your reputation (your public self) and your integrity (your private self) match. They mesh. When they don't, it's a heap of trouble and destruction. Judas was going down a slippery slope because he lacked character, ultimately leading to his demise.

From these definitions, we can conclude that integrity is concerned with and rooted in our private world. Personal integrity is validated in the hidden parts of our lives.

STRUCTURAL INTEGRITY EXAMPLE

To illustrate the depth of integrity, let's imagine a tall skyscraper in New York City, New York. When an engineer certifies that the building has structural integrity, he is not referring to anything visible. He's not talking about the height, exterior beauty, or grandeur of the building. When the engineer says the building has structural integrity, he is talking about the hidden parts of the building. Some of those hidden parts are the foundation and steel beams. The foundation of the building runs deep into the earth. The steel beams are properly placed underneath to undergird and strengthen the building. It is assumed the foundational components (support beams, columns, and slabs) are in place and well constructed when you see that beautifully tall skyscraper. Most people don't think of these elements as they walk into a building. Their focus is on the noticeable features—bricks, windows, layout, and design elements—that the public can easily see. These visible aspects draw comments, photographs, and admiration.

The average person only becomes aware of a lack of structural integrity when the disrepair is obvious to the eye. A building that doesn't have structural integrity will buckle under the weight of pressure and cause destruction. At this point, who cares about how well the building looks in photos if no one can use the building because of its instability?

The same is true for personal integrity. Your personal integrity must be sound. It must be stable because it is holding up everything else. No one will care about how well you delivered a speech and how truthful the points in the speech are when they find out that your outward life and persona are much different from your hidden actions.

A leader can have a BIG REPUTATION for being charismatic and appearing to do all the right things, but the hidden part of their life (the core, inner structure) is weak and falling apart. They lack integrity. This is why the public usually feels outraged when it's revealed that a leader they admired is caught in a scandal—especially those they held in high moral regard, like clergy members, teachers, worship leaders, nonprofit directors, coaches, and counselors. Their public and private lives did not match. Some leaders have come up short through sexual infidelity, others through financial mismanagement, and sometimes because they have exploited people. The hidden part of the leader's life often causes the leader to stumble and buckle under the weight of leadership.

Integrity matters. It is a core building block of good character. Every great leader must master the temptation not to lead a life of integrity. Because of technology (social media, apps, mobile phone cameras), gone are the days when a reputable leader could say or do something dishonest, shady, rude, abusive, disrespectful, or fraudulent and not worry about seeing all of the sordid details played out in the 24-hour news cycle for all the world to see. The old wise saying, "You can be sure your sin will find you out," and "What's done in the dark will come to the light," is almost a guarantee for today's leaders. The reality is that even the average man or woman has reason to be concerned that at any moment, their disreputable behavior might be captured in a video and go viral on social media. Who you are matters. It matters to God. It matters to those who follow you, and it should matter to you.

WHY IS INTEGRITY SO IMPORTANT?

One reason integrity is important is because integrity matters to God. **God tells us not to be so concerned about the outward appearance (big persona) but to look at the heart (inward character).** The prophet Samuel was sent to select and anoint a new king of Israel from Jesse's sons. However, God told Samuel to not look at his appearance or his physical stature. *For the LORD does not see as man sees; for man looks at the outward appearance, but the LORD looks at the heart."*[1]

Seven of Jesse's sons were kingly in appearance, height, and age so Samuel (and Jesse) assumed the new king was among them. Jesse made a big show of marching them in front of Samuel. Meanwhile, the youngest son, David, was not in the spotlight. He had been overlooked by his own family and others as he faithfully tended to his father's sheep. It never occurred to anyone that God chose him for the leadership position because he didn't seem to fit the outer, more superficial tenets of success. God looked at his heart and private life. God saw David's true essence and integrity instead. David went on to be a great king despite his mistakes because, at the end of the day, David wanted to get it right and God knew it.

Another reason integrity is important is because it is a key factor in leading others with moral authority. There are two primary ways to lead: (1) positional authority or (2) moral authority.

The person who leads from positional authority leverages the power of the position to keep subordinates (or followers) in line and to get things done. They try to motivate others through praise, reward, anger, threats, or manipulation. It's really about their own perceived importance and the task at hand. They try to get results through others by commanding them to complete tasks instead of inspiring them. Some leaders lord their position over others with statements like, "As your supervisor, I need you to…." They need to keep reminding everyone of their position because no one respects them. Other leaders aren't so obvious in their language, but the result is the same. Leading through positional authority is not character-driven.

What gets done is more important than *how* it gets done for this type of leader. In other words, you value people for what they can do, not for who they are. When you're leading from a platform of positional authority, you will create environments of insecurity and fear.

Let's contrast that with leading through moral authority. This leader's life creates respect and admiration from followers. This is why you may have a manager in positional authority, but your department gravitates to another employee or volunteer they admire. Those who lead through moral authority seek successful outcomes. However, the end doesn't justify the means for this type of leader because people and outcomes are inseparable. They are ambitious but not at the expense of mistreating people. They are thoughtful, kind, patient, and humble (refer back to the previous chapter on the *fruit of the spirit* for the full listing). They have integrity (wholeness) and are honest about their flaws. They don't blame others for their mistakes. They will admit when they are wrong. Outwardly their words match their feelings. They're not mean or brutally honest. They're just honest. This type of leader is trusted and not feared even though they hold followers accountable. The followers know the leader will not mistreat or mishandle them, even when they are being corrected. People are drawn to and want to submit to them because of who they are and how they lead. Their life creates respect so there's no need to demand it.

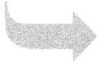 In Him was life, and the life was the light of men.[2]

It was Jesus' life that gave life to everything He did. It was His life that gave life to His teaching. His life gave life to His leadership and motivated others. It's one thing to teach about love or kindness but it's another thing when you **live** it. Others feel it. When your words and actions are character-driven and match your life, it's light to those who see it. It's attractive. Why does this matter? Because the more people follow you, the more influence you have in shining light in dark spaces.

Evaluate yourself. Are you leading others through positional authority or moral authority? Would people follow you if they didn't have to? Do you even know? Do you care? Do you mistreat others? Do you manipulate your followers or subordinates to get things done? If so, you are not leading with moral authority. This is true for staff at an organization, attendees of churches, and children who have parents who outwardly say they care about them but practically run their household through fear. When that child grows up, it shouldn't be surprising when they don't call or visit you. If you see yourself in any of these scenarios, you still have time to fix it. Go to the person(s), acknowledge your wrongdoing, apologize, and change your ways. Become a person who leads through moral authority.

The final reason integrity is so important is because it is a key factor in the longevity of your leadership. God doesn't want you to be a shining star, and all these people are drawn to your leadership and then you fade out because of a lack of integrity. This means you have BIG REPUTATION but no staying power.

I am a huge basketball fan. Whenever it's time for the NBA Playoffs or the Finals, I'm watching them. I do not particularly value the players who pop up and are great in one game. Their name is broadcast everywhere, and everyone is talking about what they did in that single game. What I appreciate are the players that are **consistent** over time. They ultimately play the most games because they have longevity. The best players are good on the court **and** have the respect of their teammates off the court. Integrity ensures you're present for the long haul. You see, Judas' leadership opportunity was short-lived. His integrity eroded and led to stealing. The stealing led to lying, and the lying led to cover-ups. The cover-up led to his death.

I pastored for 42 years and eight months. That's what I mean by longevity. Of course, I didn't do everything right. I'm the first to admit that I was not perfect. I made a lot of mistakes, but the difference was that I wanted to do it right. I wanted what people saw out front concerning me to be what happened in my private life. I wanted my public and private life to match. I wanted wholeness because that's what God looks at. He looks at the heart.

HONESTY

Since honesty is a facet of integrity, let's look deeper.

> **HONESTY** {def}:
> › a refusal to lie, steal, or deceive in any way even when it is expedient
> › refusing to cheat
>   − cheating is breaking a rule or law; gaining advantage in an unfair way

> avoiding manipulation even when you have the position and the power to do it
  - twisting words and playing on emotions; managing situations in a sneaky fashion to get what one wants
  - using one's position or influence to accomplish one's agenda with no regard for the benefit or loss of others

The first definition means that even if others behave dishonestly in a situation, you refuse to do so. The definition mentioned lying, but what is a lie? A lie is a false statement, misrepresentation, misleading appearance, or behavior. The Bible says, *"You shall not steal, nor deal falsely, nor lie to one another."*[3] There are a few different types of lies. A premeditated lie means you plan to deceive ahead of time. The hypocritical form of lying involves acting differently than what you say or claim. The silent lie does not say or offer information that should be disclosed. The exaggeration lie embellishes the facts. Finally, there's the denial lie, which is the refusal to admit the truth about something unpleasant or uncomfortable. In society, we rename sins to make ourselves feel better about them. For instance, do you justify your dishonesty by calling your lie a white lie?

The second definition of honesty is related to cheating. There are several ways that people cheat. I've listed a few examples, but there are plenty more.

- **Relationship cheating:** Physical or sexual intimacy with someone other than your spouse or with someone else's spouse.

- **Financial cheating:** Relates to dishonesty in acquiring, managing, or in the disbursement of financial resources. For example, a failure to pay income tax is a form of financial cheating.
- **Academic cheating:** Use of dishonest or unauthorized methods to achieve a satisfactory score or credit on an assignment, test, or evaluation.
- **Leadership cheating:** Undermining a subordinate's growth and development by not allowing them to face challenges or make decisions on their own.
  - Learned Helplessness — Solving a subordinate's problem cheats them out of the competence and confidence that comes from solving their own problems. When you do not allow them to solve some of their own problems, you rob them of the opportunity to develop problem-solving skills. This is true for parenting your child as well.
  - Micromanagement — Micromanagement cheats people out of discovering and developing their creativity. If you have your hands in everything, that's not support. It robs subordinates of the opportunity to shine by not allowing and encouraging them to use their own knowledge to contribute and generate value. Additionally, it cheats subordinates out of motivation because if you're handling everything, they won't be motivated.
  - Failure to Delegate — When you don't delegate, you cheat your subordinates of the opportunity to grow and

to use their talents and abilities. You also cheat them of gaining experience and expertise.

- Equal Rewards and Praise — When you reward everyone on the project team the same, you cheat your outstanding performers out of deserved affirmation, and they will become demotivated. They start to think, "Why should I spend all this time while others aren't carrying their weight?" You are also cheating your low performers of the coaching and honest feedback they need.

Now, let's talk about the third definition of honesty. It relates to manipulating others or situations. As a department head, director, line supervisor, or team leader, do you try to manipulate others into doing what you want by saying the directive or suggestion came from your supervisor when it really came from you? Or do you mention a highly respected colleague's name to sway a coworker's decisions? That's manipulative! We have to eliminate this from our leadership! Do you do this?

GEHAZI EXAMPLE

Dishonesty is related to lying, cheating, and stealing at its core. Let's look at the life of a man who lost his leadership position because of dishonesty. His name was Gehazi, and he was the servant of a powerful leader named Elisha. People looked up to him because of his close connection and position alongside Elisha in ministry.

Elisha was a great prophet of God. One day, a man named Naaman came to Elisha, seeking to be healed. Naaman was a high-ranking military official from a foreign government. He was a powerful, wealthy leader, but he had leprosy. Through a series of events, Naaman learned that the prophet of God in Israel could bring healing to him. So, he came to Elisha for help. After Elisha heard the Word of the Lord, he told the general to go dip seven times in the Jordan River, and he would be healed. Initially, Naaman was very skeptical about the prophet's instructions. However, he obeyed the prophet and was cleansed. The leprosy disappeared immediately. Leprosy was an incurable, infectious disease. Naaman was deeply grateful to Elisha and wanted to share his financial resources with him, but Elisha basically said, "You're welcome, but no, I don't want anything for myself or the ministry."

Although it would have been okay for Elisha to accept financial resources, in this instance, he didn't want Naaman to think the anointing that healed the leprosy came from anyone but God. But Gehazi (Elisha's servant who enjoyed a position of influence) saw Naaman's gratitude as an opportunity to enrich his own pocket. We pick up Gehazi's story of dishonesty and corruption in 2 Kings 5:20-27 (NLT) after Naaman leaves. I've added commentary to draw your attention to the points.

> [20]*But Gehazi, the servant of Elisha, the man of God, said to himself,* **"My master should not have let this Aramean get away without accepting any**

of his gifts. As surely as the LORD lives, I will chase after him and get something from him."

[Notice the premeditation.]

²¹*So Gehazi set off after Naaman. When Naaman saw Gehazi running after him, he climbed down from his chariot and went to meet him. "Is everything all right?" Naaman asked.*
²²*"Yes,"* **Gehazi said, "but my master has sent me to tell you that two young prophets from the hill country of Ephraim have just arrived. He would like 75 pounds of silver and two sets of clothing to give to them."**

[There are a few unethical issues here. Gehazi misrepresents that he had the authority to speak on Elisha's behalf. He lies multiple times. He also manipulates and exploits Naaman by introducing a human-interest element. In today's world, this would be like tugging on people's heartstrings to get them to donate to a charity that doesn't exist.]

²³*"By all means, take twice as much silver," Naaman insisted.* **He gave him two sets of clothing, tied up the money in two bags, and sent two of his servants to carry the gifts for Gehazi.**

[The moment he accepted money and gifts, he not only stole from Naaman, but he cheated him. Remember, cheating means to gain an advantage in an unfair way. Also, others (Naaman's workers) are being impacted by the lies. The lie created more work for them, which means Gehazi stole time from them. He only cared about what benefited him.]

> [24] **But when they arrived at the citadel, Gehazi took the gifts from the servants and sent the men back. Then he went and hid the gifts inside the house.** [25] **When he went into his master, Elisha asked him, "Where have you been, Gehazi?" "I haven't been anywhere," he replied.**

[Lies always result in cover-ups. Cover-ups lead to more deception, which leads to more lies.]

> [26] *But Elisha asked him, "Don't you realize that I was there in spirit when Naaman stepped down from his chariot to meet you? Is this the time to receive money and clothing, olive groves and vineyards, sheep and cattle, and male and female servants?*

[A consequence of lying is you lose credibility. No one believes you. People won't trust you if you lie.]

> [27] **Because you have done this, you and your descendants will suffer from Naaman's leprosy forever."**

[His family's lives are forever changed by his dishonesty and corruption.]

> *When Gehazi left the room, he was covered with leprosy; his skin was white as snow.*

[In this case, the consequence was immediate and detrimental. However, if you get comfortable in your lies because you haven't yet been held accountable for them, you will deceive yourself into thinking everything is okay. They will continue and eventually will catch up with you.]

As you can see from the story, Gehazi was dishonest in several ways. The lapse in his integrity caused him to not have longevity as a leader. Not only did it undermine his authority, it cost him his life.

Don't be like Gehazi or Judas by mismanaging your leadership stewardship. Leaders have the capacity and ability to direct and influence people, but it all begins with you working on your inner self. And developing your integrity is a terrific first step toward laying that excellent character foundation.

ACTIONS TO TAKE

1. Look at your social media timeline and activity. Does your portrayal align with your real thoughts, values, and actions? If you see that your public activity is either untruthful, leaving a false impression of who you are, or is hypocritical, take a break from posting and work through those unsupervised areas of your life to bring them into alignment.

   - Example: If you are married, do you publicly show beautiful, loving photos of your spouse with words of admiration while privately cursing them?
   - Example: Are you commenting on someone's posts saying one thing, but you're privately gossiping the opposite about them?
   - Example: Are you a financial advisor posting about putting guardrails in place for others, but you're stealing from the company you work for?
   - Example: Are you posting about your Christian values, but the comments you're making are not Christ-like to or about certain groups of people?

2. Have you recently told someone a lie? Who do you need to come clean with? Don't delay. Go to them and be honest by admitting your mistake.

3. Stop justifying your dishonesty.

CHAPTER 4

FAITHFULNESS

*'Well done, good and faithful servant;
you have been faithful over a few things,
I will make you ruler over many things...*
(FROM THE *PARABLE OF THE TALENTS*)[1]

Faithfulness is one of the character traits of the *fruit of the spirit*. I wanted to highlight it in this chapter because although there's a spiritual aspect, it is one of the practical building blocks of good character.

The Bible frequently mentions God's unwavering faithfulness time and time again. The Word shows His steadfast commitment to fulfilling His promises, even in the face of what appears to be impossible situations. Over the years, God has been so faithful to me. When He says He's going to do something, He does. I can count on Him. He is reliable because faithfulness is who He is. If you ever want to know God's nature, you should look to Jesus. He was faithful in His assignment when He was here on Earth.[2] In fact, there wasn't a single thing God asked Jesus to do that He didn't see through to the end. He is faithful even now.

Are you diligent in your assignment and purpose on Earth? Are you diligent and obedient to God and His instructions? Can you be trusted?

I think that at the heart of *faithfulness* is how committed you are to where you are and not just where you want to go. It's your faithfulness in relation to God and others. Faithfulness has three components that we want to look at closely:

- Trustworthiness
- Dependability
- Perseverance

TRUSTWORTHINESS

Trustworthiness means keeping your word. You are slow to make a promise and slow to put your word out there because you know that if you say it, you must do it. If I tell you, you can count on me. You can take it to the bank. Can people take your word to the bank? Can they rely on you? Your word should be your bond. When you say that you're going to show up, do you? When you say that you're in, are you all in, or are you inconsistent? When you agree to something, do you even believe yourself?

FAITHFULNESS

Although we covered integrity at length, I would be remiss not to mention it here. Keeping your word entails carrying out your commitments and being truthful in your communication. Being dishonest diminishes trust. Honesty creates trust, and trust is the glue to any successful endeavor or relationship.

Luke 16:10 says, *"He who is faithful in a very little [thing] is faithful also in much, and he who is dishonest and unjust in a very little [thing] is dishonest and unjust also in much"* (AMPC). Notice that it mentions faithfulness and the need for honesty in the same passage. Do what you say, no matter how tiny. If you have children, do you keep your word to them? If you say you're going to buy them a piece of candy today, do you dismiss what you promised them because you no longer feel like going to the store? Do you dismiss it because they're young and not in a position of power? Do you dishonor your agreement with them because the candy is not a big deal to you? The more you don't keep your word to them, the faster they will stop trusting you.

When I pastored, I had the opportunity to counsel married couples. There were times when one of them was guilty of infidelity. They were unfaithful. The act(s) broke their vows at its core. They didn't keep their word. The first thing to disintegrate is trust. Whoever broke the trust has a long road to rebuilding trust. For the restored marriages, it was because the offending partner developed a new consistency in being truthful. For the marriages that failed, it was because trust was lost and too many lies were told.

Are you trustworthy as a leader of your household? Or on your job? People will not trust you if you lie, cheat, or manipulate situations. How careful are you with your words? Do you lead with honesty and integrity? Just remember, if you don't have trust, you will look behind you and notice that no one is following you.

DEPENDABILITY

The second component of faithfulness is dependability. Where trustworthiness is broad, dependability hones in on your ability to be counted on by others. *Dependability* is the ability to consistently and reliably fulfill your commitments and responsibilities.

Can others rely on you to carry out your duties and obligations? If your parents, immediate supervisor, ranking officer, or professor have to be on the scene for you to fulfill your commitments, this means you are not a dependable person. Others may not have a high degree of confidence in your ability to be dependable. Do people believe they can depend on you?

A faithful leader leads themselves. They are self-motivated by the internal attitude, "I am responsible for this, and no one has to be around in order for me to complete my assignment. If they give it to me, they know it's going to get done." Being on time for appointments, meetings, and deadlines is a sign of dependability.

A dependable person who is also trustworthy will let others know if they are unable to fulfill an obligation. People don't have to hunt you down. If anything changes, they are the first person to notify others about the change and communicate it in a timely manner.

PERSEVERANCE

Perseverance is the third component of faithfulness. Have you ever met a person who just does not give up? If they've decided they are going to do something, have something, or be something, they don't quit until they accomplish the goal.

Perseverance is a refusal to quit. It is a dedication to seeing things through to completion. A person who perseveres proceeds in life like this:

- "If I start it, I'm going to see it through to the end."
- "If I begin it, I'm going to show up consistently. I'm going to show up on days that I feel like showing up. I'm going to show up on days that I don't."
- "I do not allow my feelings to dictate my choices. My feelings may decide to tag along, but they do not get to drive. My feelings do not drive my level of commitment. My feelings don't drive my level of excellence."
- "I am a faithful person."

ACTIONS TO TAKE

1. What has God told you to do? Have you been faithful in this assignment?

2. Pray and ask God to reveal areas where you lack faithfulness with Him and others.

3. If you have broken trust with someone, go to them and talk to them about it. Acknowledge it, apologize, and find out what they'd like you to do to help rebuild your relationship.

4. Before you make a commitment, stop and think, "Am I actually going to do this, or am I just saying something that I think they want to hear?"

5. Ask those around you whether they consider you to be dependable. If they respond negatively, do not become defensive. Consider this as an opportunity for growth.

6. If others have expressed frustration to you because you never arrive on time for your commitments, put technology to work for you. Start setting reminders on your computer, phone, or apps. Set the reminder with a margin for getting dressed, travel time, and unforeseen traffic delays.

CHAPTER 5

STEWARDSHIP

Stewardship is an important structural piece in building character from within. It requires a pivot in your perception that you can use your blessings however you wish. It addresses how you practically manage the time, talents, and material possessions God has entrusted you with in a way that honors God's intentions and purpose for your life.

> **STEWARDSHIP** {def}:
> › to manage or look after (another 's property)
> › the careful and responsible management of something (or someone) entrusted to one's care
> › the use of God-given resources to accomplish God-given purposes, goals, and assignments

A key to your internal growth is recognizing that you are a steward, not an owner. God is the creator and owner of every good thing. This means in your role at home, in the community, or the marketplace, you are partnering with God in His business to rear His children (not yours). You and God become partners in leading His people, executing His vision, and managing His resources. Good stewardship is the management and wise use of time, talents, relationships, opportunities, wealth, and other resources to accomplish God-given purposes, goals, and assignments.

Have you noticed in the Scriptures that stewardship and faithfulness are often linked?[1] This is because faithfulness over what you already have is the number one requirement to be entrusted with more blessings, talent, staff, and followers!

 Instead of your prayers being focused on, "God, please give me more," consider whether you're doing the right thing with what you already have.

Do you wish you had a bigger house but don't take care of the one you have? Are you praying for more money while wasting the money you already have? Do you want more children but are emotionally and physically neglecting the one you're raising? The best approach to receiving more is to demonstrate your commitment to steward what you already have.

I learned this the hard way. Our church was incredibly small at first, and it remained that way for many years. I used to say I could stand in the pulpit and throw a bowling ball in any direction and not hit a single person. On many Sundays back then, I would teach a great message and then go home and cry over the poor attendance. It felt like people were staying away in droves, yet I knew God had told me to start the church. I was discouraged and frustrated. I often complained privately to God about the church not growing. Finally, one day, the Holy Spirit quickened a Scripture in my Bible, 1 Corinthians 4:2: *"Moreover, it is required in stewards, that a man be found faithful."*[1] I had an inspired thought to be faithful over the members I had. The harsh reality I had to face was God revealing to me that I was a bad steward. I was so focused on what I didn't have that I was mismanaging the individuals He had sent me. I wasn't loving, caring for, or tending to the people who were coming. I realized that you could become ungrateful about what you do have. It was in those days that I learned the difference between needing people and loving them. I needed numbers as a leader; I needed them to make me look good. The more people, the better I'd look publicly. Once the Lord gently corrected my perspective, I realized I was "despising small beginnings."[2] I began to see my leadership as stewardship, which meant each person's growth and care were important even if no one else came. My part was not church growth. That was God's part. My part was good stewardship. I learned to see each congregant for who they were. This was another opportunity to help and serve.

THE SCOPE OF STEWARDSHIP

The scope of stewardship includes at least eight areas. Everything you and I possess and everything we are belongs to God. Let's look at this list to see the eight primary areas of stewardship.

- Spirit, Soul, Body[3]
- Word of God[4]
- Purpose[5]
- Talents, abilities, and gifts[6]
- Time[7]
- Relationships/People[8]
  - Family, children, followers, employees, congregants, clients, subordinates
- Positions/Roles
  - In the world[9]
  - In the Church[10]
- Material Wealth[11]

Are you partnering with God to produce, increase, and multiply these resources for His kingdom, or are you neglecting them?

DON'T BE DECEIVED

"Moreover, it is required in stewards that one be found faithful."[12] This implies that God, the owner, makes the determination on whether you're being faithful or not based on

the instructions He has given you. Scripture also tells us that God will require each of us to give an account of ourselves.[13] This means all of us should see ourselves as stewards of God's resources. It doesn't matter if your work is in a secular career field or the Christian mission field, you are a steward of that assignment in the Earth. You—*the teacher, plumber, doctor, lawyer, law enforcement officer, military sergeant, administrator, business leader, computer technician, engineer, nurse, pharmacist, seamstress, chef, mother, father, student, or minister*—are God's steward, and He will hold you accountable for your stewardship. It is a deception to view those activities and responsibilities through any other lens.

An area of stewardship that is often neglected is stewardship of our family and home life.[14]

Leader, you have an obligation to prioritize your family in terms of your time, energy, money, and emotional support. It doesn't matter if your title is apostle, bishop, pastor, deacon, worship leader, or children's worker. Your job or volunteer role does not take priority over your family. This trap of poor stewardship of your family is one that many Christian leaders fall into. I must admit I fell into this trap as well. I had corrected the way I stewarded the congregation, but while doing so, I found myself constantly tending to their needs (hospital visits, funeral services, counseling appointments, ministerial support, sermon preparation) at the expense of my family time. I had become a bad steward of my family. I would frequently get up from the dinner table to answer urgent calls. I hadn't set boundaries. Wrong priorities will not only destroy your family, there is great potential for misplaced priorities to also destroy your ministry. Once I realized I was out of balance, I started blocking my calendar every Monday to be with my wife. It was her day, and I started spending more time with our children.

Some of the mistakes many Christian leaders make in the mismanagement of their family stewardship are:

- Not satisfying their spouse's needs
- Reckless disregard for the importance of their spouse's needs
- Ignoring or not valuing the role of their spouse and children in their success
  - Failing to prioritize and develop a meaningful connection with their children
- Leaving their spouse and children off their calendar
  - Failing to schedule family time that is completely unrelated to church or ministry

Simply working to maintain a good reputation is not stewardship. A good reputation is important, but it is not a substitute for good character. Proper management of stewarding your leadership is a distinctive mark of building the practical side of character.

ACTIONS TO TAKE

1. What gifts and talents has God entrusted you with? Make a note of them.

2. Are you using those talents and skills to help others? If not, start now.

3. Are you being a good steward of your time? Write down how you are wasting this essential resource. Determine what you need to prioritize to regain more of your time for what you're supposed to be doing.

4. Have you asked God what your purpose is?

5. As a leader, are you being a good steward over the people God sent you? Or are you using them for your own purpose to complete *your* goals or to make you look better? Be honest with yourself. If you only care because you need them, then you're a poor steward. What can you change today?

6. Did you notice any adjustments you should make in stewarding your leadership? It's not too late to act now.

TRAIT TWO

PIVOT FROM BIG STARTS TO
DISCIPLINE

"It was character that got us out of bed, commitment that moved us into action, and discipline that enabled us to follow through."[1]

ZIG ZIGLAR

CHAPTER 6

YOU MUST BE DISCIPLINED

If you want to start anything worthwhile, you must have a plan to execute it. Let's say your goal is to lose 20 pounds. Your plan may include downloading a calorie tracker, buying a kitchen scale, studying nutritious foods, and going to the gym twice a week. You can envision your clothes fitting differently. You are confident that you will succeed because you have done your research in advance. You are ready to start! But once you start following a nutritious diet and exercise regimen, the actual work of it causes you to give up.

There are leaders who have BIG STARTS. They have a wealth of enthusiasm and energy towards their new project or initiative. They appear to be "all in," but these BIG STARTS end with the same results as an **incomplete pass** on a fourth down in a football game. No yards gained, no points added to the score, and the other team now has control of the ball. Ultimately, when this continues to happen, the goal of winning is not achieved.

There are also great leaders who experience longevity in their careers, get things done, finish what they start, and avoid scandal and moral failures. Those leaders are disciplined people. You must become a disciplined person if you want your life and your leadership to inspire and influence others and have the support of people who are willing to take the next step with you. If leaving a legacy that can be respected is your goal, you must become a disciplined person. I challenge you to pivot from BIG STARTS to having self-discipline.

What is self-discipline?

1. Self-discipline is the ability to make yourself do the thing you need to do when it ought to be done whether you want to or not.
2. Self-discipline is the strength not to do the things you want to do that contradict godly values and hinder you from fulfilling your destiny.
3. Self-discipline is the mental and emotional strength to commit to doing or achieving something, maintain focus, and resist impulses until the thing is finished.

These definitions offer different sides, facets, and shades of meaning. We'll delve deeper into the third definition later. However, the first two definitions go hand in hand. On the one hand, you know there is a task you must do, when you must do it, and you do it regardless of how you feel at the moment. Imagine how much you could accomplish if you could just do that! What are you supposed to be doing that you're not doing?

I'm reminded of John C. Maxwell saying, "Success depends not merely on how well you do things you enjoy, but how conscientiously you perform those duties you don't."[1] How conscientiously do you perform duties that you don't want to do? This is so important because when you face pain and pressure, you will give up on your goals unless you have self-discipline.

On the other hand, self-discipline is about having the strength not to do things you know you shouldn't. This is critical. Self-discipline is critical to the longevity of your career as a leader.

THE APOSTLE PAUL

The Apostle Paul had a BIG START. He had a life transformation when he encountered Jesus on the road to Damascus, wrote 67% of the New Testament, was caught up to Heaven and shown the future, took part in the supernatural healings of the sick, and experienced the manifestation of the Holy Spirit working through him in all manner of gifts of the Spirit. So yes, he had a BIG START, but he also had a big finish and that should be every leader's goal. Many leaders make a big show about starting but never finish. Like in our football illustration earlier, they make one incomplete pass after another right when the game is on the line. Paul didn't do this. He completed his assignment on Earth. He completed the purpose God gave him. He finished what he started. But how? He gives us the secret to his success:

> *But I discipline my body and bring it into subjection, lest, when I have preached to others, I myself should become disqualified."*[2]

He says he disciplines himself. That's his secret. Notice that he says he disciplines himself so he doesn't become disqualified. I don't like that word *disqualified*. I don't want to be disqualified. What about you? The word *disqualified* means "to be declared ineligible; ineligible to compete, ineligible to perform, ineligible to operate in a certain area, or to continue to participate in an area because one has done something wrong."

This concept applies across a spectrum of environments. If you're an employee, you can disqualify yourself and get fired because of substance abuse. Multiple traffic violations can disqualify you from legally driving. They will suspend your license. As a manager, harassment toward another employee can disqualify you from receiving a promotion, keeping your job, or even result in more severe consequences. If you're an athlete and disobey the rules, you will be disqualified from participating in the sporting event. In politics, lying about your credentials can disqualify you from public service. And in ministry, cheating and stealing can disqualify you from leading.

You can disqualify yourself through moral and character failures, lawbreaking actions, rule-violating behaviors, and more. Thank God, I have good news today! You have control. You can avoid disqualification by disciplining yourself!

Paul talks about discipline and tells us that in his human tendencies, "dwell no good thing."[3] If he disciplined himself so that he wouldn't become disqualified this means that there were things that he wanted to do that he should not do. Likewise, there were things that he did not want to do that he should do. He didn't trust his body to align with God's Word and his values. As a result, he told his body what to do and what not to do.

I don't want to be disqualified! This is why I practice self-discipline. I want to be transparent with you and share the good, the bad, and the ugly of my leadership journey. A few decades ago, there were things my flesh wanted to do that would have contradicted my godly values. I desired things that would have hindered me from fulfilling my destiny, but I was honest with God and shared my temptations with Him. He said to me, "Ask me for more grace." I did, and He gave me the strength to face the temptations. Imagine if I had not disciplined myself. The stewarding of my leadership would have either ended, or I would have lost my effectiveness and credibility as a leader. Both are detrimental. I am sure that I am not alone in having to discipline my flesh and tell it, "No." In fact, none of us are alone. We share the same struggle as the great Apostle Paul, and we have the same Jesus Who *"always causes us to triumph"* in Him.[4]

The Word of God gives us the answer for how to overcome the weaknesses of the flesh. It says His grace is sufficient to strengthen us when we are weak.[5] Rest in His grace. This means you have the ability to be self-disciplined!

ACTIONS TO TAKE

1. Think back to the last thing you started. Did you accomplish what you set out to do? Did you complete it?

2. Write down one task you've been procrastinating on and do it this week, even if you don't feel like it.

3. If you have had BIG STARTS but have failed to see them through, go back to those who were impacted and apologize to them. Do better for your next initiative.

4. Become a self-disciplined person by doing the things you know you should be doing when you should be doing them and not doing the things you know you're not supposed to be doing.

CHAPTER 7

YOU MUST COMMIT

The Apostle Paul advised Timothy to *take heed (to give serious attention) to yourself* and then to the doctrine.[1] Therefore, self-discipline must be a component of leading yourself first so you can inspire and influence others. Our third definition of self-discipline provides an overview of the practical steps required to succeed.

> **SELF-DISCIPLINE** {def}:
> › the mental and emotional strength to *commit* to do or achieve something, maintain *focus*, and resist impulses *until the thing is finished*
>   – (This means to discipline yourself you must **commit**, **focus**, and **finish**.)

Let's cover the first step. You must commit. But what is a commitment?

> **COMMITMENT** {def}:
> › a firm, strong, calculated *decision* to do something
> › the state of being *bound* emotionally, intellectually, or spiritually to some course of *action*

When you commit to a goal, you are making a firm decision. The Latin root of the word "decision" is to *cut away from*. So, what you're really doing is you're cutting away all other options when you commit. You're cutting away all excuses. Commitment is a firm decision to cut off everything that does not aid you in finishing the course of action you've started.

BURN THE SHIPS

The following is a classic historical example of what I've just explained about cutting away all options. Hernando Cortez invaded the Mayans in southwest Mexico in 1541. As they climbed the mountains toward the Mayan villages, the soldiers looked back and saw smoke on the beach. Cortez had instructed the few remaining soldiers on the beach to burn the ships. His instructions were, "When we get to the mountains, I want you to burn the ships." In burning the ships, he reduced the possibility of anyone deciding to turn back. Eventually, they won the battles, but think about that. He had the soldiers burn the ships they had arrived in. This left them with only two options: (1) fight and win or (2) fight and die here. Tucking their tails and running was not an option. Have you truly made a commitment? Have you burned the ships? If you're going to be a great leader, you're going to have to burn some ships. I'm sure you're thinking, "Well, I'm just too busy. I have a lot on my plate. I don't have time." If you're going to develop your leadership capacity, you're going to have to cut away all the other options and all of the excuses. You're going to have to make a commitment.

BOUND TO ACT

If you are engaged to be married, this means you have made a commitment to eliminate all your other dating options except for your fiancé. When you're in a committed relationship, you are cutting yourself off from other options. A commitment—whether it's in relationships or in other areas—is more than a verbal declaration of "I do" or "I will." Notice the definition talks about *being bound* to the action. This means you are tied to acting on your decision. This is powerful. Commitment is not just a state of mind. It requires action.

 Commitment starts in the unseen parts of our being, but it must be followed with action that can be seen.

If you have committed yourself to taking care of an elderly parent, you must follow through by doing so. If you have committed to the community that you will fight for their rights, then you must act on it. You have cut away all other options, and you are bound to it emotionally, intellectually, or spiritually, no matter what it costs you. Psalm 15:4-5 paraphrases it this way: that you should "swear to your own hurt." It encourages you to follow through on your promises, convictions, and commitments despite the possibility that it would be tough or painful to your flesh, require self-control, be an inconvenience, or cost extra time or money to do it.

This brings to mind the story of the chicken and the pig. One morning, they were discussing breakfast and what they were committed to doing to make it happen. The chicken said, "I am committed to giving one egg every day." The pig scoffed at her use of the word commitment. He said, "That's not commitment. That's just participation. I'm providing the bacon. Now that's commitment." This was an extreme example, but it helps to drive home the point that true commitment involves some level of sacrifice. You should always count the cost before you make a commitment.

DELAYED GRATIFICATION

Let's talk about self-discipline as it relates to commitment. Self-discipline is not an event but a process. It requires commitment. A commitment is a continuous process of choosing delayed gratification over instant little rewards. It's not a commitment until it is tried and tested. Jesus Christ, the greatest leader to ever walk the Earth, understood this principle. We see evidence of delayed gratification in the context of preparation versus action. Most of us, (and I'll lift my hand), want to choose action over preparation. That is a problem! That's why we often enter arenas that we are not qualified for and ultimately disqualify ourselves because of the lack of preparation. Preparation isn't fun. Preparation can be hard spiritually, mentally, emotionally, relationally, physically, and financially.

For the first 29 years of His earthly life, Jesus was in preparation. He began His ministry at the age of 30. After being prepared for 29 years, He changed the world in just three years. Over 2,000 years after His death, we are still being impacted by His leadership. He chose preparation. He chose delayed gratification. He chose to sit in the temple, listen, and ask the religious leaders questions as they were astonished at His understanding. He had an appreciation for His call to leadership, but He still went home to His parents and submitted to them. It was a season of preparation. It was not time for Him to enter leadership. He disciplined Himself.

 If you have gifts and talents, it can be easy to move straight to action. When you have a calling on your life, you will be tempted to skip steps so you can get to the instant gratification step. Don't! You must understand that preparation **always** precedes action.

EXAMPLES

Remember, self-discipline is a "continuous process of choosing" delayed gratification as it relates to commitment. To discipline yourself, you will need to shift your attitude from an event-oriented mindset to a process-oriented mindset. This is easier said than done! Here are a few examples.

Let's revisit our example of losing weight. If eating more nutrient-dense, healthy foods and losing weight is your goal, you must be committed to it. It's a process. You are continuously choosing to do it. You have counted the cost. It will take time, energy, restraint, and more. If you have an event-oriented mindset, the moment the scales show that your weight hasn't budged (or worse, you've gained a few pounds), you will be tempted to abandon your hard work and sacrifice because of the belief that "it's not working anyway." This would lead you to start searching the internet for a magic pill to fix it all. You can't do that! It's a process! Yes, self-control can be hard, but you made a commitment to yourself to permanently change your nutritional and exercise habits.

Now, let's say you're a businessperson or aspire to own a business. In this season, you may really want a financial breakthrough. Instead of looking for money-making schemes to get quick income, decide to commit to providing value to your clients and to your customers day in and day out. Don't skip steps. Don't jump to immediate gratification.

PUT DISCIPLINE TO WORK

Before deciding to commit to an endeavor, determine what cost is involved. How does your commitment impact your team or followers? Your decision means you've cut away other options and the commitment has now bound you (or realistically your team) to an action. When you truly understand this, you will have insight into making better decisions on anything you choose to commit to. It's like giving discipline a job. You're able to put it to work for you to perform duties and responsibilities. You are in control of your words and where you direct your attention, time, energy, and resources when you possess self-discipline. Self-discipline means you're the boss of discipline! Although discipline has a simple job description, it doesn't mean it's easy. But knowing what you need to decide, establish, and manage will help you to count the cost more accurately **before** you commit yourself.

DISCIPLINE'S JOB DESCRIPTION

1. Decide, establish, and manage my **words**
   - **what** I say
   - **when** I say it, and to
   - **whom** I say it.

   Because an undisciplined tongue can trap me into making more commitments than I can keep.[2]

2. Decide, establish, and manage my **attention**
   - **what** gets my attention
   - **when** something gets my attention, and to
   - **whom** I give my attention

   Because what I give my attention to, I will desire.[3]

3. Decide, establish, and manage my **time**
   - **what** gets a portion of my time
   - **when** I give an unplanned portion of my time, and to

- **whom** I give an unplanned portion of my time
Because time is a non-renewable resource; once it's gone, it's gone forever.[4]

4. Decide, establish, and manage my **energy**
   - **what** levels of my energy I give and what levels I keep
   - **when** I should level up in giving my energy, and to
   - **whom** I give priority when my energy level is low
   Because energy is a renewable resource that can be leveraged to cover deficits in many things including time, resources, and skill.[5]

5. Decide, establish, and manage my **resources**
   - **what** gets allocated a portion of my resources
   - **when** to reallocate certain portions of my resources, and to
   - **whom** my resources are allocated and devoted
   Because resources are assets which must be properly and diligently managed in order to get the most out of them.[6]

OVERCOMMITMENT

Discipline's job description starts with your **words**. The disciplined leader decides, establishes, and manages what they say, when it's said, and to whom it's said. This means you have discipline over what you say "yes" to and what you say "no" to. Self-discipline helps you avoid overcommitting yourself. Much of the time, this is where the BIG START with an incomplete pass begins. You may have already made a commitment to do something, but then other things that you find important—whether it's one huge task or a bunch of smaller tasks—start fighting for your attention. As a leader, I know you can relate! Those additional commitments come from every direction!

If you agree to new commitments, your words have now overcommitted you, and you wind up losing vital attention, time, energy, and resources, which results in not finishing what you started. As a leader, you failed to employ discipline to manage your words.

FOOTBALL ANALOGY

It's sort of like in football when the defense calls a play to rush the passer in the red zone (the area inside the opponent's 20-yard line). In this scenario, the drive has been successful. The offense has advanced the ball down the field, is positioned in the red zone to score a touchdown, and reads the defensive play as a normal, base defense. Everything looks normal. The quarterback is in the pocket, set, waiting for the snap, and ready to make the pass. He has the skills to throw the football accurately, and he has talented receivers ready to catch it. So, the touchdown is basically a done deal, right? Wrong!

Remember, the defense plans to rush the passer. That means that the quarterback will have several 300+ pound players coming at him full speed while he is attempting to get the football to a receiver in the end zone. At the line of scrimmage, the defense looked like they were set up in a normal, base defense. But, right before the snap, the defense changes the play at the last second to blitz (surprise attack) the quarterback.

Suddenly, one side of the offensive line is facing more defenders than it can block because the defense loaded that side with more defenders than normal. The quarterback calls an audible to defeat the defensive strategy. The blitz fails. It is one thing for the defense to call a blitz, but leaders can blitz themselves with overcommitment.

When a leader commits to another big thing over here or a few small things over there, there are too many things coming too fast. The blitz of commitments will rush the leader with overlapping and competing timelines. You've committed yourself—and, by extension, your team—to more than you should. You've allowed overcommitment to put you in the position of making a BIG START that will force a fumble, result in a sack, or create pressure that ends in an incomplete pass. How demotivating for the team to put in all that hard work to advance the ball down the field (it took their attention, time, energy, and resources), but there were no points to show for it at the end of the drive.

If this pattern keeps repeating itself, how motivated do you think the team will be to get set up at the line of scrimmage for the next BIG START? How many more times do you think the team is going to have confidence in your ability to manage the game? If the quarterback is the undisciplined leader and repeatedly adds more commitments, how much blocking should he expect from the offensive line? We've all seen games where it "seems" like the offensive line missed a block on purpose and the quarterback got hammered.

This book is about pivoting from outward success to inward growth. You must do the inner work! Self-disciplined leaders embrace the concept of commitment, and then they commit, but they don't overcommit. Legendary football coach of the Green Bay Packers, Vince Lombardi, is widely quoted as saying, *"The quality of a person's life is in direct proportion to their commitment to excellence."*[7] A commitment to excellence within the context of what we're talking about means to excel in discipline in terms of how you allocate and manage your words, attention, time, energy, and resources.

You don't want to end up getting hammered because your team stops blocking for you. It will hurt if you lose the support that you once had because you won't make the pivot to discipline your words and commitments. You will not be able to motivate your team to take the next step with you if they are fed up with the BIG STARTS that usually end in a lot of work, effort, and sacrifice from them but with an incomplete pass. People like to win. Whether it's winning the game or winning the drive by putting some points on the board, people want to win. Of course, winning the game is the goal, but I have found that they will keep playing if they have small victories along the way. However, nobody wants to keep playing when they're not scoring at all, and nobody wants to keep playing if you appear to be playing for the defense against your own team!

Make the leadership pivot from BIG STARTS to discipline. Even if you've had a losing record and are actively in the process of rebuilding your team, you will find yourself completing more passes and putting some points on the board if you lead with discipline. If you go even further and become **disciplined in your FOCUS**, you will eventually start winning some games and your team will still be right by your side.

ACTIONS TO TAKE

1. Do your commitments mean anything to you? Take a moment to really think about it.
2. Stop skipping the preparation period and going straight to action.
3. If you make a commitment, be bound to act.
4. Get to the root of the problem and resolve it. If you are overcommitting yourself and your team members, which leads to the incompletion of commitments or a lack of excellence in fulfilling the commitments, ask yourself, "Why am I overcommitting?"
   - Are you doing it for people-pleasing reasons?
   - Are you sabotaging yourself and those who follow you?
   - Going back to the chapter on faithfulness, do you have a dependability issue that you need to fix?
5. If you're unsure whether you're overcommitting those who follow you, consult with a team member who you know will be honest with you. During the conversation, avoid being defensive, and do not dismiss their feedback. If you do, you will not grow.

SPECIAL WORD TO PASTORS

I want to talk to the **pastors** who are reading this book. Since I have pastored for over 42 years, I know something about the joys and challenges of pastoring. Commitment is a process for you, not an event. I've always said, "Pastors don't get discount tickets." You must apply God's Word and business principles, just like your followers. Instead of looking for a simple formula or a seemingly magic solution, commit to focusing on educating yourself as a leader. Develop a team around you, and care for those you already have. Commit to doing the last thing the Lord told you to do. Commit to doing your part. While I was worrying years ago, the Lord told me, "Do your part. Rest. And the church will grow." If while you're reading this you're thinking, "Studying leadership sounds good, but I don't have time for that, just show me how to make the church grow," then you have an event-oriented, magic-solution mentality. You need to change that. You've been praying for God to grow your church, but God will not send you a bunch of people if you are not prepared to lead those people. He will not send you hundreds or thousands of people right now because they will fall through the cracks because you don't have a team or infrastructure in place to care for them. Remember, just like the Lord loves you, He loves those people, too.

CHAPTER 8

YOU MUST FOCUS

*But Jesus told him, "Anyone who lets himself
be distracted from the work I plan for him
is not fit for the Kingdom of God."*[1]

Many leaders today find it increasingly difficult to focus on what matters most. I want to emphasize that many of *us* leaders find it increasingly difficult to attend to or focus on what matters most. I don't know about you, but I'm on my leadership journey and it is a challenge to stay focused.

It has been a challenge from day one. Even after all these years of leading, I still find it difficult to focus and attend to what matters most. It's difficult but not impossible. It requires self-discipline. Remember, self-discipline is *the mental and emotional strength to commit to do or achieve something, maintain focus, and resist impulses until the thing is finished.*

When I'm talking about maintaining focus, I'm referring to focusing on what you're supposed to do and not on distractions. The fact that you must maintain it means it's not automatic. Leaders who lead with discipline are not easily distracted because **they** control their focus.

A distraction is anything that takes your focus away from what you are supposed to be doing. A distraction is anything that gets you to turn aside from God's commands, plans, and His Word. The law of distraction states, *"The more distractions we have, the less we achieve."* Why is this true? It's true because energy flows where attention goes, and what we focus on gets bigger. Therefore, the more distractions we have, the more diluted our focus becomes. Energy flows away from the goal and towards the distractions because that is where our attention is. Distractions are expensive. They cost us valuable time and energy. Remember, discipline's job description includes managing your words, attention, time, energy, and resources.

There are multiple biblical examples of those who lost focus, and it cost them dearly.

1. Samson was anointed and called by God, but the stewarding of his leadership ended prematurely because he became distracted. Samson's distraction was women. Eventually, he allowed himself to be totally distracted by a woman named Delilah and it was his downfall. Notice, I did not say that she was his downfall. The "it" being referred to is the distraction that was his downfall. Allowing himself

to be distracted because he was undisciplined prematurely ended his role as the leader of God's people.

2. Adam and Eve became distracted. Eve became distracted by the serpent. Adam became distracted by his wife, and they both turned aside from what God had commanded and planned. They both turned aside from God's Word.

3. Demas is another person who became distracted. He was a minister of the Gospel, a leader in the church, and a co-laborer with Paul. However, he left the ministry because he *"loved this present world."*[2] Distraction weakens our resolve to persevere and ultimately finish.

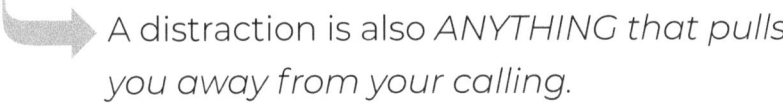 *A distraction is also ANYTHING that pulls you away from your calling.*

All of us have a calling. God has a purpose for everyone. There is something that God has designed for you to do on the Earth, and only you can do it. If you get distracted, it could delay your journey.

If you think about leadership, distraction is *anything that pulls you away from your leadership responsibilities.* You can steward your leadership in various arenas: at home as a parent, spouse, or sibling; at school as a student leader; at work; or in other sectors such as business, the military, politics, education, or athletics.

PARABLE OF THE SOWER

In Mark 4, Jesus teaches a parable that we call the Parable of the Sower. He says the farmer went to sow seeds, and some seeds fell by the wayside. Some seeds fell on stony ground. Some seeds fell on thorny ground, and some seeds fell on good ground. In verses 18 through 19, He introduces distractions.

> *"Now these are the ones sown among thorns; they are the ones who hear the Word, and the **cares of this world**, the **deceitfulness of riches**, and the **desires for other things** entering in choke the Word, and it becomes unfruitful."*

He explains that there are three categories of distractions: (1) distractions of the mind, (2) distractions in our priorities, and (3) distractions of our time. The "cares of this world" are the distractions of the mind. They include the mental health struggles that cause you to be pulled in different directions in your thinking. You can't be an effective leader and worry at the same time. If you're full of worry or anxiety, it destroys your ability to focus. Also, the "cares of this world" can include being weighed down by responsibilities. Many of these responsibilities are legitimate responsibilities like, having a job, running your household, or managing your team.

Jesus introduces us to distractions from our priorities. He called these "the deceitfulness of riches." The word *deceitful* here means delusion, a false appearance (something that attracts us with the false promise of reward and pleasure). The deceitfulness of riches, which also means 'false blessing,' is an open door that God did not open. Let me clarify here. He's not saying riches are bad. He's warning about how riches can be misleading because of economic pursuits that pull you away from what you're supposed to do.

These economic pursuits would include a job offer, promotion, business opportunity, or even an educational goal that pulls you away from God or pulls you away from your family. When you prioritize economic pursuits over God, family, relationships, church, and everything else, you're out of balance. When you're working so hard to get money that you can no longer spend time with your children, it's a problem and a distraction.

I've taught for years that God wants us to be successful in every area of life. A part of being successful is to develop our minds as far as we can along with developing our spirits. Development is good, but do not allow it to distract from your priorities.

God's Word should be the foundation for your leadership. You should base your decision-making, actions and reactions, plans, and strategies on biblical principles. When you lose focus, it will become an issue for you and those you serve.

PRACTICAL EXAMPLES OF DISTRACTIONS

Here is a list of things that can dilute your focus. I have a personal connection to most items on the list below. I have a college degree. I watch television. I attend meetings. I enjoy sports. I'm active on social media. So, we're not talking about sin or terrible things, but things that can easily pull you away from what God called you to do.

Your job
Your career
Too many meetings
Too much volunteering
Mental and emotional cares (i.e., worry, anxiety)
Relationships
Overly focused on other people and their issues
Business ventures
Opportunities
The pursuit of riches
The pursuit of degrees and credentials
The pursuit of popularity through likes, followers, and subscribers
Social media
Gaming
Talking on or using apps on your cell phone
Binge-watching TV and streaming services
Your social life
Sports
Push notifications

You must recognize these distractions for what they are and fight them because they will be ongoing. The level of your discipline combined with the level of your commitment to overcome these distractions and maintain focus will determine your level of success as a leader.

ACTIONS TO TAKE

1. Ask a trusted friend, coworker, or family member to show you areas in which you are imbalanced.

2. Revisit the practical examples of distractions list from this chapter and determine if you are allowing any of these things to pull you away from your goals. Now that you're aware, make a change.

3. The next time you're having a face-to-face conversation with someone, count the number of times you look down at your phone because you received a push notification, email alert, or text message. Mentally decide not to shift your focus to your phone. This will strengthen your connection with the person.

4. Are you doing *good* things instead of *God* things? If so, make the adjustment. Read Luke 10:38-42. Martha focused on legitimate responsibilities (or *good* things), but Mary focused on what was important—the Lord.

    - God wants you to have an integrated life. Workaholism is symptomatic of an undisciplined life. Are you a workaholic? If so, carve out time to do things you find important that are non-work related. Fight the urge to work.

5. Ask God what your purpose in life is if you don't already know. Wait for His answer.

6. Take steps to pursue what you're supposed to be doing. Focus.

CHAPTER 9

YOU MUST FINISH

The Apostle Paul committed and focused, and he finished his course.[1] What a testimony! Disciplined leaders FINISH! Remember, our third definition of **self-discipline** is the mental and emotional strength to commit to do or achieve something, maintain focus, and resist impulses until the thing is finished.

FINISH {def}:
› To arrive at or attain the end of, to bring to an end; complete.
› To accomplish; to reach the goal; to carry to completion; to bring to a successful conclusion.

Running a race gives us an easy example of what it means to finish. My daughter runs 10K races and marathons. As she runs, she must fight the urge to quit due to course complications or physical exhaustion. The same is true for leading yourself. You must prepare mentally and physically to endure the journey. Resist the impulses so you can finish what you started.

I want to give you seven mindsets you must adopt to be a leader who finishes what you start. Feel free to say these out loud so you hear yourself. Make the pivot!

1. Doing *good* things rather than *God* things will cause me not to finish. I must do *God* things.

2. Taking on need-based causes that have not been assigned to me by God will cause me not to finish. There will always be needs coming my way, but I will not be able to focus if I'm always finding a need and filling it. I can provide support to those who do have a mandate to fill certain needs, but I must stay focused on and be faithful to **my** God-given assignment, and **my** course.

3. Impatience will cause me not to finish. I must resist the emotional impulses that tempt me not to wait on God's timing.

4. God has blessings and a good plan for my life. My part is to commit, focus, and prepare myself to be a good steward of His blessings.

5. Workaholism will cause me not to finish. God blesses the work of my hands, and I should not have to toil.

6. Worthy but untimely opportunities will cause me not to finish. God gives opportunities to His people, but I must resist the temptation to accept an opportunity that does not fit my condition, value system, resources, the season that I am in, or my vision.

7. Growth and increase without discipline will cause me not to finish. I believe that God wants me to grow and increase in every part of my life. I understand that growth and increase come with more opportunities to be distracted and unfocused, so I am committed to developing my capacity to recognize distractions and properly manage my focus.

Being self-disciplined takes work! You must control your emotions, resist your impulses, watch your words, restrain your reactions, be committed, focus on what's important, and finish the race God has set before you. In any race, a good start is important, but nobody remembers the start. It's your finish that counts! When you practice self-discipline, your leadership abilities will grow.

Start with yourself. Be the leader by whom others will be inspired. Develop a plan to accommodate people's needs. Discipline yourself, and people will notice.

ACTIONS TO TAKE

1. What have you started that you need to finish? Take steps today to finish.

2. Be honest with yourself.
   - Just as you're making progress on your goal, do you have a pattern of self-sabotage that causes you not to finish?
     – What impulses are causing you to continue to have incomplete passes?

3. What *good* things have you said "yes" to that you need to now say "no" to in order to get back on course to the finish line? It's not too late to make a course correction.

TRAIT THREE

PIVOT FROM BIG SHOT TO
HUMILITY

"The greatest among you must be a servant. But those who exalt themselves will be humbled, and those who humble themselves will be exalted." [1]

— JESUS CHRIST

CHAPTER 10

PRIDEFUL LEADERSHIP

Nobody wants to be led by someone who thinks they are a BIG SHOT. You know, that person with an overinflated sense of self, a superior view of themselves and their abilities, and frequently displays arrogance. They are constantly telling others how important they are and about their accomplishments. I'm sure you've run into this person before. This leader, whether they are overtly prideful or more subtle, can be frustrating to submit to.

PRIDEFUL LEADERS:

- have a spirit of independence and a stiff-neck (stubborn) attitude, making it difficult for them to yield to God or others (THIS IS A MAJOR PROBLEM).
- inordinately take pleasure in the power that comes from a position or title. They're quick to let you know who they are. You can't accidentally call them Mr. or Ms. Smith.

They correct you immediately with "I am Dr. Smith" or "I am the head of this." They are very conscious of their actual or perceived status. You sense that air about them—that need for power and control to feed their confidence.

- always need to be right and everything must be done the exact way **they** want it. It's their way or the highway.
- overestimate their abilities and underestimate the skills and efforts of others because they inherently think their abilities are superior. In downplaying what others bring to the table, they erroneously believe it enhances their own image.
- struggle to accept criticism and constructive feedback. They reject feedback because it would be admitting they don't know it all, and it challenges their sense of superiority. Also, accepting suggestions for improvement would mean they need to improve. They don't think they need to improve.
- blame others or those on their team and refuse to accept responsibility for their own failures. We call it 'throwing people under the bus'.
- take credit for team success. The team does this and then all they talk about is themselves. How **I** did this. How **I** thought of this. How **I** came up with this. They do this because they have an inflated sense of self importance.
- use people's skills to further their own ends and not to build relationships.

- can't admit mistakes. They can't even acknowledge them when it's abundantly clear to everyone that they made one.
- are competitive and need to be better than others, even against their own teammates, which reinforces their sense of value.
- refuse to accept help from others.
- exhibit hurtful, insensitive, demotivating behavior towards others.
  - This can include openly treating others as inferior, belittling them, or talking down to them in a condescending or dismissive manner, which undermines the person's confidence and value.

Most prideful leaders will not exhibit all the listed traits and behaviors. However, they check off many boxes.

PUT PRIDE ASIDE

If you recognize yourself, please know to become a leader that others will want to follow, you **must** put pride aside and pivot from being a BIG SHOT to humility. It is mandatory! **Humility is the opposite of pride.** It is an awareness that one's security is in God. A humble leader puts God's interests before their own. They recognize and respect the gifts and abilities of others since they are not focused on themselves. Without pride, they can see how different each person is and genuinely appreciate their contributions.

In the workplace, it is essential to recognize that others may have superior skills and growth potential. While you might possess talents, others might excel in specific areas. Instead of insisting on completing tasks out of pride, operate with humility. In other words, pivot from being a BIG SHOT. Step aside and allow others to showcase their skills. By doing this, you motivate others to strengthen their skill set and encourage the team to trust and value each other as you lead by example. This creates a domino effect that makes everyone feel eager to contribute with their skills because they feel valued.

 The best executive is the one who has sense enough to pick good men to do what he wants done and self-restraint to keep from meddling with them while they do it.[1] — *Theodore Roosevelt*

In the early stages of full-time ministry, my wife and I did everything in the church. We cleaned the building and took care of the grounds. As the church began to grow, the demand became even greater. More people were willing to help. Even though I had a certain way that I liked those tasks to be completed, I had to allow other team members to take over handling the church grounds so I could concentrate on preparing and delivering the sermons. I could not micromanage the team who agreed to clean the church building because my task list grew. I had to humble myself and allow them to contribute in a way that would help everyone.

Years later, I led church strategy meetings. I noticed the wisdom that my business school graduate son, Michael K. Moore, had during those meetings. He would give great ideas and ways to execute them. It was incredible to watch. Although I was ultimately in charge, I recognized my son was extremely intelligent in strategy. It takes humility to recognize that someone else you've raised and mentored is better at certain things than you. Once I realized that, I turned the church strategy sessions over to him going forward. It was a win-win because he came up with projects, initiatives, and strategies that I would have never come up with alone. Humility allows others to shine, and it opens the door for partnership.

Proverbs 29:23 states, *"A man's pride brings him low, but honor shall uphold the humble in spirit."*[2] Refusing to put pride aside hurts you, but pivoting to humility promotes growth.

QUALITIES THAT DEMONSTRATE HUMILITY

1. Look beyond status. Consider people over titles, and do not allow rankings to dictate how you treat others.
2. Don't be selfish. Prioritize the needs of others.
3. Intentionally learn about those you lead, who they are as a person, their needs, and perspectives.
4. Believe that everyone is valuable and deserves respect.

5. Consider yourself a steward and not an owner of people. Your role is to guide and support them.
6. Have a deep concern for others and their success.
7. Recognize and celebrate others' gifts, skills, and talents.
8. Be servant-hearted by serving others rather than seeking to be served.

Remember, the traits of a prideful leader? **To operate in humility, do the opposite of what the prideful leader does!** You cannot influence anyone who doesn't respect you. No one respects a prideful leader. When you're operating in pride, you have a disconnect in your leadership. Everyone else (including your followers) sees it except you.

ACTIONS TO TAKE

1. Ask yourself:
   - Do I think I'm a BIG SHOT?
   - In what ways has pride crept into my leadership?
   - Since I may have a blind spot, do I have someone I can ask if they see signs of pride in me? NOTE: You need an advisor. See Chapter 13, "Courage to Lead," for a list of advisor types.

2. Check your conversation. Do you say things like, "It will not get done if I don't do it," "I am the only one who can do things right around here," or "Everything would fall apart if I did not show up for a day"? This may reflect that you believe others can't succeed without you, which may be rooted in pride.

3. When was the last time you took credit for something someone else did? Go to that person and apologize.

4. Take inventory. Re-evaluate people and their skill sets to determine who is good at certain tasks or wants to learn a task. Then, provide the opportunity and space for them to grow in that area. NOTE: You are not doing this to prove your skills are better than theirs.

5. Just be honest with yourself and make the necessary adjustments. God doesn't want you to feel condemned. He wants you to humble yourself, fix it, and grow. Pride is a spiritual issue. Ask Him in prayer for His help.

CHAPTER 11

LISTEN TO OTHERS

*"... Everyone should be quick to listen,
slow to speak..."*[1]

A part of pivoting from BIG SHOT to humility is learning how to listen to others. What does listening have to do with humility, and why is it important? When someone comes to talk to you, and you already think that what they have to say is unimportant or that you already know what they are about to say, you will not be open to hearing them. To take it a step further, if you believe that your way of doing a task is the best way, you will view others' opinions and feedback as a waste of time. You must first be humble and willing to hear and truly consider what others have to say.

IMPORTANCE OF LISTENING:

1. Listening is the key to learning.
2. Listening is the key to understanding people.
3. Listening helps you see your personal blind spots, such as areas of weakness, ignorance, personality flaws, leadership style flaws, and sometimes decision-making weaknesses.
4. Listening keeps problems from escalating.
5. Listening shows that you care.
6. Listening creates trust and engagement.
7. Listening helps you as a leader to comprehend the situation.
8. Listening helps you minimize miscommunication.
9. Listening provides a broad perspective and communicates respect for others' expertise and experience.
10. Listening is a prerequisite to obeying God.

A staggering study of 14,000 employees worldwide revealed a disheartening truth: only 8% of them considered their mid- to senior-level leadership to be good listeners.[2] Even more alarming, a 2020 employee study found that 1 out of 10 employees lack trust in their manager's willingness to listen to their complaints.[3] As a leader, your ability to inspire, connect with, and align those around you is heavily dependent on effective communication. At the heart of communication lies the crucial skill of listening. Yet, both research and reality show that this skill is sorely lacking in most leaders.

Moses was a great leader. His father-in-law, Jethro, spent

time with him and the Israelites when they were in the wilderness. He noticed that the people came to Moses to resolve their disputes and receive wisdom, forcing him to sit all day resolving them. Jethro explained that this was not a wise use of his time and instructed him to teach the people the commands of God and identify men within those groups that he could train to resolve the disputes between the people. Those men would be trained to lead groups with different amounts of people, between ten to thousands. This would allow Moses to do other things, and not just counsel all day. Moses listened to his father-in-law's advice.[4]

 Moses' survival in the wilderness was not just a result of his resilience but also his humility.

He could have easily dismissed Jethro's counsel and even argued that Jethro had never done anything like this before. However, as a humble leader, he accepted the feedback. This act of humility allowed him to value the contributions of others by simply listening.

FEEDBACK

Excellent leaders listen to feedback. Valuing employee, volunteer, and customer feedback is demonstrated by you creating a system for collecting, evaluating, and using it. If you understand that feedback comes in many forms and that all of it can improve your organization, school, or community, you will look for it more.

Although this list isn't exhaustive, consider these areas when requesting feedback from those you lead:

- Ideas to improve the organization
- Observations concerning the climate or culture
- Feedback concerning the individual needs of team members

As a pastor, I had to be willing to make that pivot and listen to my team, those within the congregation, and others around me. On one occasion, I had to be open to feedback when a member of my congregation came to me after I had preached a sermon and told me that I could "talk better" and use better grammar. Instead of getting upset, I listened to what she was saying and enrolled in an English class at a local college. I must admit that it helped me become a better speaker.

CONSEQUENCES OF NOT LISTENING

There are consequences to not listening with compassion to those following you. Rehoboam was made king after his father, Solomon—who was considered the wisest king in history. The people came to Rehoboam and told him they wanted to continue serving him but requested that their workload be reduced. King Rehoboam consulted two groups of advisors. The first group of advisors had served his father, Solomon, well. Their advice was to give the people what they requested and speak kindly to them because they said it would encourage them to serve him forever. He then consulted the other group of advisors, his peers. They advised him to make their workloads harder, increase their punishments, and speak harshly to them. This was the opposite of what the people had asked. He took the advice of his peers and did not listen to the wisdom of the elder advisors. He increased people's workloads. The people revolted, and ten tribes left, leaving him with only two tribes.[5]

In other words, the followers walked out because their leader refused to listen. Leadership plays a crucial role in maintaining workplace morale. When leaders fail to listen to their employees, it can lead to a company culture with low morale and high turnover rates. Employees who feel undervalued and mistreated are unlikely to stay, especially after voicing their concerns to leadership. When people speak, they want to be heard, and it's the responsibility and privilege of a great leader to listen. You must have big ears!

ACTIONS TO TAKE

1. On a scale of 1-10 (with 10 being an outstanding listener), how good of a listener are you?
   - Ask others to rate you using that same scale. (Do not get defensive.)

2. Do people feel comfortable coming to you with quality feedback?

TRAIT FOUR

PIVOT FROM BIG WIMP TO
COURAGE

> "I learned that courage was not the absence of fear, but the triumph over it. The brave man is not he who does not feel afraid, but he who conquers that fear."[1]
>
> NELSON MANDELA
> *(Former President of South Africa)*

CHAPTER 12

BE BRAVE, CONQUER FEAR

The Bible tells us the story of Joshua. He was a military leader and a skilled warrior. Moses sent twelve spies to explore the Promised Land. Ten of the spies came back fearful and discouraged, but Joshua and Caleb came back energized and gave a positive report despite the overwhelming obstacles others feared. They encouraged the people to have faith that God would give them the victory. When Caleb said, "We are well able to overcome it," Joshua agreed. In Joshua 1:6-9, God has chosen Joshua to succeed Moses to lead the people (thousands of them) into the Promised Land. With Moses gone, he had big shoes to fill. This new leadership role had its own challenges and the tasks were daunting. Joshua felt the weight of his new responsibilities. In verse nine, God gives him instructions and encouragement. The fact that He commands it means it's possible.

> *"Have I not commanded you? Be strong and courageous. Do not be afraid; do not be discouraged, for the Lord your God will be with you wherever you go."*[1]

As a leader, you must possess courage. The Greek philosopher Aristotle called courage "The mother of all virtues because without it, you cannot consistently perform the others."[2] The same can be said about leadership; you cannot lead without courage. Just like Joshua, you will be required to make bold and often unpopular decisions and dismantle traditions. Are you up for it?

WHAT IS COURAGE?

Courage is the ability to act despite fear, adversity, danger, or difficulties. Courage gives you the confidence to lead in the face of adversity. That is why you need it. As a leader, adversity shows up, and you must be able to stand firm, or you will crumble. **Leadership is not for wimps.**

LEADING WITHOUT COURAGE

WIMP {def}:
> (noun) a person who is not strong, brave, or confident
> (verb) to fail to do or complete something as a result of fear or lack of confidence

God gave Saul very specific instructions through the prophet Samuel. God said to follow His commands completely and destroy everything from the enemy they defeated. Once they won the battle, Saul didn't obey. At first, Saul claimed he obeyed when Samuel confronted him about this. Then he tried to shift the blame onto his soldiers, and eventually, he admitted he disobeyed because he was afraid of the people and gave in to their demands.[3] Saul buckled under pressure rather than following God's command. His decision revealed his lack of courage and poor leadership skills. Rather than leading with boldness and sticking to what was right, he let fear of others' opinions and pressure from the people influence his actions. He was a wimp. Are you a wimp? Do you see any of these characteristics in yourself?

CHARACTERISTICS OF A WIMPY LEADER

- Makes a lot of excuses — afraid to take ownership
- Avoids conflicts — afraid of being hurt, rejected, or feeling uncomfortable
- Procrastinates — afraid to make mistakes
- Follows the pack — afraid to stand out
- Is a people pleaser — afraid to upset people
- Isolates themselves — afraid to be vulnerable or exposed

A wimp is afraid, afraid, afraid. I dealt with several of these characteristics when I first became a pastor decades ago. To be honest with you, I was a wimp. I was a people pleaser, a procrastinator, and I avoided conflicts. That was not healthy, and I realized that wanting to please people is what Joyce Meyer calls an approval addiction.[4] When pleasing people becomes higher on your agenda than leading people, you are no longer helping them. Thankfully, I began to grow, and that growth started with self-evaluation and being honest. I realized that unresolved issues of past hurts and feelings of rejection were negatively affecting the way that I was leading. I had to get a handle on that, because I wanted to be better which would make me a better leader.

LEADING WITH COURAGE

If you notice any of these characteristics in your leadership, do not be afraid because you can pivot yourself from being a BIG WIMP to leading with courage. Our great example of a courageous leader is Jesus. In Luke 4:18-20, He said, *"The Spirit of the Lord is upon Me, Because He has anointed Me To preach the gospel to the poor; He has sent Me to heal the brokenhearted, To proclaim liberty to the captives And recovery of sight to the blind, To set at liberty those who are oppressed; To proclaim the acceptable year of the Lord."* Then He closed the book, and gave it back to the attendant and sat down. And the eyes of all who were in the synagogue were fixed on Him.

He basically stood boldly in front of his hometown crowd and said, "I am the One Isaiah prophesied about" and went and sat down while they stared at Him. The people did not like that at all and considered it blasphemy. Jesus had to make a decision. He knew what He said was true, even though it was not being received well. Many of them were upset and others dismissed Him because they knew His parents. He had to be bold and say what they did not want to hear to be able to lead them to the truth. He had to deal with the criticism of others and stand out front despite their thoughts of Him. You need to follow His example. Be brave!

CHARACTERISTICS OF A COURAGEOUS LEADER

- Refuses to compromise principles, values, and convictions for profit, growth, or prestige

    ○ At one point, I was asked to use my influence to encourage members of my church to purchase a product that promised to help them save money on their phone bills. Along with saving money, our church would also receive a percentage of those sales. While there is nothing wrong or illegal about that offer, I declined because it did not align with my principles and personal convictions concerning how to use my influence from the pulpit.

- Exhibits boldness to speak up when their opinion or perspective is unpopular

    ○ I did a sermon series years ago called *When Color Doesn't Matter* on race relations, and I wrote a book in

2020 entitled *Muted Voice: A Challenge to the Body of Christ to Speak Out Against Racism*. Honestly, I dealt with a lot of backlash because it was an unpopular opinion. Yet, I had to stand courageously because it was a message that needed to be heard. Ultimately, it helped so many people.

- Is willing to let go of traditions when they no longer work
  - Traditions can be programs, groups, or activities that are done, but you see that they no longer have the impact they once had. Letting go of certain programs within the ministry was difficult because that usually meant telling the person who was leading it that we were not doing that anymore. I always had to be aware of when it was time to let go of traditions, as changes in people, seasons, times, and situations signaled the need for change.

- Has the strength to face difficult and uncomfortable conversations head-on
  - The difficult conversations are exactly that—difficult. Although they are never easy, it was an important part of my role. It can be addressing a simple violation, explaining a change of plans, or firing someone. The level of difficulty should not stop the conversation from taking place. Build up your courage and deal with it correctly.

- Seeks and receives unfiltered feedback
  - I have had to provide a safe space for others to give me unfiltered feedback to help me learn, improve, and change. To do that, I created an atmosphere where people felt comfortable talking and being honest with me because they knew that I valued what they said. The feedback has helped me on numerous occasions.

- Embraces diversity
  - Working with different people allows me to have different perspectives. I have been able to work with people with viewpoints, knowledge levels, and ethnicities different from my own. This allows me to see things in new ways, which makes me a better leader.

- Asks for help
  - I am happy to receive help from people who have a skill set that I do not have. It is better for everybody that I get help instead of trying to do those things myself. This has never been a problem for me. However, if you fear what others may think of your lack of knowledge, it may take courage for you to push past this and ask for help.

- Says "No"
  - There were times when I felt like I had to say "Yes" when the honest answer was "No." There can be a fear of letting people down. I learned that saying "Yes" is

worse when I know the truth is "No." (i.e., turning down speaking engagements or having to reject someone's idea.)

- Admits mistakes
  - I have stood before my congregation and honestly admitted when I made a mistake. Having so many eyes looking at you when you are in such a vulnerable state is not fun, nor is it for wimps. But when I was honest about my mistakes, people would come and thank me. It increased their confidence in me as a leader.

- Shows genuine emotions
  - Do not be afraid to cry. Things will affect you. It's fine to show your emotions. They don't disappear just because you're a leader. I've given many eulogies for church members whom I loved. I have watched people grow and achieve goals that made me happy to see and it brought tears to my eyes. That was okay because I am not a robot, and neither are you.

As I grew as a courageous leader, I made mistakes along the way. I learned from them and continue to be better. It has taken courage for me to lead, but that is why I can continue on this journey. Trust me, you do not want to be a wimp; you will quickly find that if you do not pivot yourself from being a BIG WIMP to courage, you will be a leader who is being led instead of a leader who is leading. Do not be afraid; be courageous.

ACTIONS TO TAKE

1. If a courageous leader refuses to compromise principles, values, and convictions for profit, growth, or prestige, do you know what yours are? Write out your principles, values, and convictions.

2. If you see yourself in any of the characteristics of a wimpy leader, courageously admit to someone that you need help in this area.

3. Take one courageous step each day toward becoming the leader you were meant to be. Whether it's taking responsibility for a mistake, standing firm in a decision, having a difficult conversation or setting boundaries with others. Do something now!

CHAPTER 13

COURAGE TO LEAD

As you continue on your leadership journey, you will be so thankful that you made the pivot from being a BIG WIMP to courage because it will affect every area of your leadership and your personal life. Since you understand why you need courageous leadership, let's look at how it will help you lead. Courage will allow you to stand out front, embrace responsibility, accept accountability, and make tough decisions.

STAND OUT FRONT

As a young man, I shied away from leadership roles because I did not want to stand out front and be seen by everyone. Standing out front puts you in direct fire for criticism and scrutiny. It puts you under a microscope and then shines a spotlight on you. When I was a pastor, people commented on everything from my clothes, shoes, sermons, and every decision I made.

You must understand and accept this. Courage allows you to stand out front with confidence and not be intimidated by all of the eyes intently watching you.

EMBRACE RESPONSIBILITY

A leader is ultimately responsible for the final results. Yes, even if you delegated the tasks or projects to others. You must embrace this. You can't blame others. As a four-star general and former U.S. Secretary of State, Colin Powell explained, "Share the credit, take the blame, and quietly find out and fix things that went wrong."[1] That can be a scary thought to many people but not to a true leader. You must work to set benchmarks, maintain communication, and assess your and others' performances to ensure that everyone can have what they need to do the job correctly. It's your responsibility.

ACCEPTING ACCOUNTABILITY

This area has two meanings. **The first is being accountable to others for your decisions.** I have found that this is a great safety net to have in place because it puts you in a position to hear what others are saying. You'll avoid making emotional decisions and be positioned to receive quality input when dealing with situations. I had a Board of Directors that decided my salary, and I voluntarily had an independent firm audit the ministry's finances yearly. These accountability measures allowed those following me to be more comfortable because of the transparency this produced. This means intentionally putting advisors in place to assist you. I recommend five types of advisors (keep in mind that one person can serve as more than one type of advisor):

- **Expert Advisor** — a credentialed person who has studied a given area in depth, understands its variations, and can walk you through it.
- **Experienced Advisor** — someone who has been in your situation, a similar one, or a more difficult situation than the one you're facing.
- **Sounding Board Advisor** — someone you trust and to whom you can reveal, in depth, what's going on.
- **Partner Advisor** — a colleague, staff member, or maybe an employee who has a vested interest in the organization's success.
- **Spiritual Advisor** — someone who can give you counsel that aligns with the Bible and can share the spiritual implications of your decisions.

The second aspect of accountability is holding others to the same standards you set. As a leader, you must ensure that everyone meets those expectations, including yourself. Failing not to hold even one person accountable can undermine your authority. Whether it's a negative attitude or poor performance, if you lack the courage to address these issues, it will impact morale.

MAKING TOUGH DECISIONS

A tough decision means taking a risk, which implies the possibility of loss or failure. Every decision has unavoidable consequences. One of those natural consequences tends to be misunderstandings with others. Courage gives you the confidence to make those tough decisions.

This pivot from BIG WIMP to courage will allow you to lead in a way that brings success and longevity.

ACTIONS TO TAKE

1. If you do not have advisors, use the guidelines in this chapter to find them. Even though I listed five types of advisors, one person can fill two roles. Once you get them, listen to them.

2. Get comfortable making decisions and hold yourself accountable.

TRAIT FIVE

PIVOT
FROM BIG TALK TO

COMPETENCE

"Well done is better than well said."[1]

BENJAMIN FRANKLIN

CHAPTER 14

TALK LESS, GROW MORE

When someone is full of BIG TALK, it means they tend to make bold claims that lack substance or concrete results. Their words and enthusiasm are impressive or ambitious at first glance, but their lack of follow-through means they are inconsistent or have no evidence to back up their words.

The root issue goes back to our first trait, pivoting from BIG REPUTATION to good character. They are more focused on creating a superficial impression on others than actually delivering on what they say. Their empty words and promises are a lack of integrity, which damages their credibility. Another reason a person may do this is because they are insecure about their abilities, so instead of being humble and admitting it, they distract everyone by sounding like they know how to do the task. Whether the BIG TALK is because of a desire to elevate themselves, a fear of failure, the need for approval, or reluctance to learn, grow, and develop, it's problematic! As a leader, it is frustrating for your followers. Eventually, they will choose not to follow you.

Do you remember our leadership definition? It is *the art of inspiring people to do something with a focus on people while delivering good results.* You won't be able to inspire anyone with just BIG TALK, and you certainly won't be able to deliver good results.

 What if you spent less time talking about what you can do and more time becoming the person who can do it?

Stop focusing on BIG TALK and start demonstrating competence, which is the ability to do something successfully and efficiently. To do this, you must embrace a growth mindset and be open to learning. You must pivot! Let's talk less and grow more.

HAVE YOU STOPPED LEARNING?

A growth mindset is a set of guiding principles inside your personal value system that consistently motivates you to keep learning. Have you stopped learning? A leader with a growth mindset wholeheartedly believes their talents, intelligence, and abilities can be further developed. They assume there will be constant change and progress. If you don't have this mindset, then I can guarantee you are stagnant. This means you're not advancing.

God wants you to continue moving to the next level in both spiritual and natural arenas: from glory to glory,[1] from faith to faith;[2] bear fruit, more fruit, and much more fruit.[3] The biblical position on growth is very clear. You and I should be learning throughout our lives. Have you plateaued in your learning?

There are two sides to growth as a leader: personal and corporate growth (of the group, team, marriage, family, organization, etc.). If you are a church leader, you need to grow to have your church grow. If you're a business leader, you must grow for your business to flourish. If you're a team leader and you want your team to grow, you must also grow. As the leader, why do you have to grow to see the "thing" grow? Because your church, business, team, marriage, family, or organization can only rise to the level you're on.

If you want to grow, you can. Growth is a function of your *want* to grow. Are you motivated to grow? There is nothing and no one, not even God, that can force you to grow as a leader if you don't want to. However, one of the innumerable great things about our great God is that **He will help you to want to**. The New Living Translation of Philippians 2:13 says, *"For God is working in you, giving you the desire and the power to do what pleases him."* Your development pleases God. Your fruitfulness pleases Him. He wants you to continue moving forward and upward from one new level to the next one in your leadership journey. A leader with a growth mindset truly believes that their talents, intelligence, and abilities can be expanded because they know they are gifts from God.

A competent leader leads with intentionality. Intentionality simply means that they don't think that personal growth is automatic or that it will just come naturally. They realize that progress requires effort. They know they must assume ownership of their growth. You must assume ownership. I am not waiting for somebody to push me. I'm not waiting for somebody to demand that I become competent in certain areas even though I'm the leader. No, I'm taking ownership of my own growth, and I'm asking God to help me.

At Mike Moore Ministries, I lead a beautiful team of godly, skillful, intelligent, and committed people, and I want them to grow with me. I've challenged them to take this leadership journey with me because I want us to **be** what we teach as an organization. I don't want to be teaching something, and my team and I are not walking in it. I want us to **be** what we're selling. I've challenged them to grow by reading leadership books, listening to my podcast, and practicing the principles they are learning. As I coach and mentor them, I encourage them to grow just like I'm encouraging you to grow.

Are you intentional about growing, or are you of the mindset that you don't have to learn anything new because you're a leader? Is your approach to leadership steeped in a mindset that you don't have to take any classes, and you don't have to listen to anybody because you have arrived? No, there's no such thing as arriving because leadership is not a destination. It's a lifelong journey. If nothing else, you will be leading yourself for life.

There are no silver bullets. You are not going to wake up one morning and suddenly know things. There's no magic formula that's going to make everything work together and produce good results without an intentional effort on your part to learn and grow. If you really want the Lord to answer your prayer about taking you to the next level, you must be intentional about acquiring new knowledge and new skills.

John C. Maxwell communicated a growth regimen[4] that I think is incredibly practical. I recommend that you consider adopting his regimen for yourself and explore his resources for further leadership tips.

He said,

- I read daily to grow in my personal life.
- I listen daily to broaden my perspective.
- I think daily to apply what I've learned,
- I file daily to preserve what I've learned.

I read, I listen, I think, and I file daily. WOW! That's intentional. I listen to other leaders often because I do NOT want to operate out of my perspective *only*. By the way, that's a mindset that will work against you as a leader. As Christians, we know the Bible gives us some absolutes, and I will never *ever* compromise those things. However, in my decades as a leader, I have found that many things are simply personal preferences. Don't allow tradition to keep you from broadening your perspective.

Tools and techniques evolve over time, requiring you to adapt to stay effective, efficient, influential, and inspirational as a leader. If you're still relying on outdated methods, it might be time to embrace something a little more current. For instance, using a flip phone as your primary device (even though they're making a comeback), sending faxes instead of emails, or not having a professional presence on social media are outdated. Even God says, *"Behold, I will do a new thing"* in you.[5]

Great leaders have a hunger for more. Why? Because times, people, situations, cultures, and methods change. We have to keep growing as bosses, parents, and community leaders. There will always be something new to learn and more to know.

Leader, you and I don't have the luxury of not advancing. Growth, knowledge, and skill are non-negotiable for us because we are out front. People come to us looking for answers, direction, and guidance. Fortunately, no matter how intelligent you are or how long you have been in leadership, there will always be others who know more than you know. That's a good thing! We'll talk more about that in the next chapter.

ACTIONS TO TAKE

1. Commit to having a growth mindset today. Own it. Be intentional!

2. Identify an area of improvement and set a clear goal that challenges you to progress in that topic.

3. Seek out advice from people you admire who are knowledgeable. Listen to them and act.

CHAPTER 15

KNOWLEDGE AND SKILLS

"Leadership and learning are indispensable to each other."
Former President John F. Kennedy[1]

After completing my pastoral assignment, I have transitioned to Mike Moore Ministries. In this season of my leadership journey, part of my assignment is to teach the body of Christ on a universal level. The other part of my assignment is to coach and mentor. Next-level assignments require new knowledge and new competencies. This means I must be willing to learn new things. I'm excited!

 What you knew yesterday got you where you are today. What you learn today will determine your success tomorrow.

Remember, competence is the ability to do something successfully and efficiently. We previously discussed that you must change your mindset. However, the next step is to DO!

We all know people who are incompetent in their job or position. Although the person is nice, they simply cannot do the job. This is NOT useful. Is this you? Have you been walking around with BIG TALK but you can't back it up with competence? Good news! You can overcome this. I've found four approaches to learning that have served me well. You must embrace all four.

1. Education
2. Example
3. Experience
4. Revelation

EDUCATION

When you learn through education, you are learning through intentional engagement using reliable sources of information. This approach gives you more control than any other. You can pursue formal education like going to college or getting certifications in your field, doing coursework, attending training events, seminars, and more. Education also includes reading books and listening to how-to podcasts. Nowadays, you can learn anything if you have access to the internet. Search out what you need to know and practice it. This would include looking on YouTube for applicable videos and searching Google for articles.

EXAMPLE

Another approach is to learn by example—by observing others. If you want to learn how to do something, watch how a skilled person does it. I'm a student at heart. When that person communicates, I listen to them. When they display talents in something I'm not knowledgeable in, I watch what they're doing and take notes. My actions are intentional. I observe how they approach it. The good thing is this person can be someone you know personally, or someone you're watching from afar.

My father in the faith was Dr. Frederick K. C. Price. He was the founder and pastor of Crenshaw Christian Center, located in South Los Angeles, California. He was known nationwide for his *Ever Increasing Faith Ministries* broadcast, which aired weekly on television and radio. As a young Christian, God connected me to him spiritually. It was a very long time before I had the privilege of being in his presence physically, but every chance I got, I observed him. I watched him on television. I studied his approach through his books and audio series. I listened to his life stories. I acquired a lot of knowledge and skills because of him. You'll be absolutely amazed at what you can learn by observing other leaders, paying close attention, and being present in the moment.

EXPERIENCE

The third learning approach is experience which means to learn by doing. When it's time to learn how to drive a car to get your learner's permit, you can first learn by education. You can prepare by studying the manual and taking practice quizzes. You can ace the written exam. You can even watch your parents drive the car every day for years, but until you get behind the wheel yourself and practice, you will not acquire the skills you need to pass the road test and become a licensed driver. So, you are still incompetent at driving a vehicle. Head knowledge will only go so far.

You need experience. It is so important for you to take what you're learning and not just make a note of it but apply it. There are times that you won't know what you don't know until you've tried it. At that point, you'll know what gaps you have in your learning. You'll know what adjustments you need to make to become skilled in that discipline. Whether you do or do not have a leadership title or position right now, you can practice leadership at work, at home, and in your community.

REVELATION

The final learning approach is through revelation, which means to learn from the Holy Spirit. Be open to the Spirit of God. He is the greatest teacher. When He reveals new ways of doing things to you, listen and apply them. The role of a pastor is a leadership role, so I needed to have leadership skills. However, the most important technical skill I needed as a Bible teacher was the ability to teach the Word of God effectively. Although I graduated from college, I did not go to seminary or Bible school. As a result, I didn't have formal education in teaching God's Word. When I first began the ministry, I used a few approaches to learning, but I asked God to help me and He was faithful to teach me. I learned quite a bit (and still do) by revelation.

START TODAY

What is a core skill set that you need in your role as a leader? Are you competent? Would others say you're competent? If you are a business owner, what functional skills do you need to take your business to the next level? Are you actively obtaining knowledge and sharpening your skills? You need to improve your skills whether you are a doctor, lawyer, government official, teacher, graphic design artist, producer, author, publisher, military official, mother, father, husband, wife, or social media influencer.

I practice what I am telling you to do. Since I'm a public speaker, developing and improving my communication skills is a core function. I consciously practice the pace and tone of my voice when speaking to family, staff, or a waiter at a restaurant. Part of communication is learning, so I practice active listening because great leaders have big ears. That's what a commitment to competence looks like. What is your own list of "must haves" for continuing your functional skill set?

I want to be clear: to be an effective leader, you don't need skills in every functional area you oversee. Yes, you may have ultimate responsibility for an area, but you can hire people to perform tasks that are not part of your core functions (SIDE NOTE: You need to be humble enough to admit you need help.) The question you must ask yourself is: *In my role as a leader of "X", what functional skills do I need to demonstrate competency?* Whatever your answer is, get skilled in that discipline. Start today. According to an old proverb, "If a craftsman wants to do good work, he must first sharpen his tools."[2] Sharpen your skills! Competence in terms of knowledge is about information. Competence in terms of skill is about ability. In your leadership role, you need both. As you commit to an investment of time, energy, and resources to grow as a leader, you will pivot from BIG TALK to competency. Those who follow you will be grateful even if they don't tell you.

ACTIONS TO TAKE

1. Commit to competency by finding a class, training, or webinar and enroll in it.

2. Is there someone who is already skilled at something you lack skill in? Identify them and observe how they perform the tasks.

3. Apply the information that you learn.

CONCLUSION

I want to thank you for taking the time to read this book. You have allowed me to be a part of your leadership journey that focuses on your personal development. Now you know why shifting your leadership focus from outward success to inward growth is so important. When **you lead yourself first**—by developing good character, having discipline, being humble, having courage, and being competent—you are naturally going to become the type of leader that many will WANT to follow. **This is how you will inspire, motivate, attract, and lead others.** You create environments in which people feel safe, valued, and motivated to grow.

So, as you take this next step in your leadership journey, keep in mind that being perfect is not the goal! Focus on one trait at a time. You've exhibited a willingness to learn. Now, **apply** the principles in this book.

You've got everything you need to make the **BIG pivot**. If you do this internal work, you will undoubtedly transform your family, community, and world. Keep me posted on your progress by visiting the contact page on my website, mikemoore.com, or by emailing mmm@mikemoore.com.

NOTES

For your convenience and further study, I have included a detailed list of citations for each chapter. I have made every effort to attribute any quotations or ideas to the appropriate person, publication, or website. Any source links or references provided were active at the time of the initial publishing of this book. For Scriptures, unless otherwise noted, please refer to the New King James Version (NKJV).

Chapter 2. Good Character Is Spiritual
1. Galatians 5:22-23 (KJV)
2. Galatians 5:22 (AMP)
3. Habakkuk 3:17-18, 2 Corinthians 8:2
4. Mark 4:38, Philippians 4:6-7 (NLT)
5. Luke 2:46, 52
6. John 15:4-5

Chapter 3. Integrity
1. 1 Samuel 16:1,7
2. John 1:4
3. Leviticus 19:11

Chapter 4. Faithfulness
1. Matthew 25:23
2. Hebrews 3:2 (GW)

Chapter 5. Stewardship
1. 1 Corinthians 4:2 (KJV)
2. Zechariah 4:10 (NLT)
3. 1 Thessalonians 5:23
4. 1 Corinthians 4:1
5. Ephesians 2:8-10
6. 1 Peter 4:10
7. Psalm 90:12; Ephesians 5:15-17
8. Genesis 18:19
9. 1 Corinthians 7:20-24
10. 1 Corinthians 12:18; Ephesians 4:16
11. Deuteronomy 8:17-18
12. 1 Corinthians 4:2
13. Romans 14:7-12
14. 1 Timothy 3:4-5

TRAIT 2 — DISCIPLINE
1. Meier, J.D. *«Zig Ziglar Quotes.»* Sources of Insight. Accessed February 18, 2025. https://sourcesofinsight.com/zig-ziglar-quotes/

Chapter 6. You Must Be Disciplined
1. QuotesWise. n.d. *"John Maxwell Quotes — Page 3."* Accessed March 10, 2025. http://www.quoteswise.com/john-maxwell-quotes-3.html.
2. 1 Corinthians 9:27
3. Romans 7:15-25 (KJV)
4. 2 Corinthians 2:14 (KJV)
5. 2 Corinthians 12:9 (KJV)

Chapter 7. You Must Commit
1. 1 Timothy 4:16
2. Proverbs 20:25 (MSG)
3. Genesis 3:6 (KJV)
4. Ecclesiastes 3:1

5. Isaiah 40:31; Galatians 6:9
6. Proverbs 21:5, 20
7. BrainyQuote. n.d. *«Vince Lombardi Quotes.»* Accessed March 10, 2025. https://www.brainyquote.com/quotes/vince_lombardi_121318.

Chapter 8. You Must Focus
1. Luke 9:62 (TLB)
2. 2 Timothy 4:10

Chapter 9. You Must Finish
1. 2 Timothy 4:7

TRAIT 3 — HUMILITY
1. Matthew 23:11-12 (NLT)

Chapter 10. Prideful Leadership
1. Theodore Roosevelt, quoted in Goodreads, accessed April 17, 2025, https://www.goodreads.com/quotes/147036-the-best-executive-is-the-one-who-has-sense-enough
2. Proverbs 29:23 (KJV)

Chapter 11. Listen to Others
1. James 1:19b (NIV)
2. Morgan, Jacob. "Research Shows Only 8% of Leaders Are Great Listeners." LinkedIn Pulse. Last modified May 7, 2020. https://www.linkedin.com/pulse/research-shows-only-8-leaders-great-listeners-jacob-morgan/.
3. Emtrain. *Emtrain Culture Report 2020*. March 2020. Accessed February 18, 2025. https://emtrain.com/wp-content/uploads/2020/03/Emtrain-Culture-Report-2020_Full.pdf
4. Exodus 18:13-24
5. 1 Kings 12:1-19

TRAIT 4 — COURAGE
1. Encyclopedia Britannica. "15 Nelson Mandela Quotes." Britannica. Accessed February 18, 2025. https://www.britannica.com/list/nelson-mandela-quotes.

Chapter 12. Be Brave, Conquer Fear
1. Joshua 1:9 (NIV)
2. Aristotle. AZQuotes.com, Wind and Fly LTD, 2025. https://www.azquotes.com/quote/482113, accessed March 10, 2025.
3. 1 Samuel 15:1-26
4. Meyer, Joyce. 2005. *Approval Addiction: Overcoming Your Need to Please Everyone*. New York: Warner Faith.

Chapter 13. Courage to Lead
1. Goodreads. 2025. "Share the Credit, Take the Blame, and Quietly Find Out What's Wrong." *Goodreads*. Accessed March 6, 2025. https://www.goodreads.com/quotes/10402375-share-the-credit-take-the-blame-and-quietly-find-out.

TRAIT 5 — COMPETENCE
1. The Franklin Institute. "Benjamin Franklin's Famous Quotes." The Franklin Institute. Accessed February 18, 2025. https://fi.edu/en/science-and-education/benjamin-franklin/famous-quotes.

Chapter 14. Talk Less, Grow More
1. 2 Corinthians 3:18
2. Romans 1:17
3. John 15:1-2, 5
4. Maxwell, John C. *The 15 Invaluable Laws of Growth: Live Them and Reach Your Potential*. Center Street, 2012.
5. Isaiah 43:19

Chapter 15. Knowledge and Skills
1. Kennedy, John F. "Speech at the Dallas Trade Mart." November 22, 1963. Accessed February 18, 2025. https://www.jfklibrary.org/archives/other-resources/john-f-kennedy-speeches/dallas-tx-trade-mart-undelivered-19631122.
2. Goodreads. 2025. "If a craftsman wants to do good work, he must first sharpen his tools." *Goodreads*. Accessed March 6, 2025. https://www.goodreads.com/quotes/7244563-if-a-craftsman-wants-to-do-good-work-he-must.

ABOUT THE AUTHOR

Mike Moore is the Founder and CEO of Mike Moore Ministries, dedicated to empowering believers to lead in their homes, businesses, ministries, and communities. Through teaching, church development, and coaching, he equips individuals with biblical truths to thrive spiritually, physically, mentally, relationally, and financially.

Mike is also the founding pastor of Faith Chapel, a non-denominational church he led for over 40 years, growing it from a small group in Birmingham, Alabama, to a multi-site ministry of thousands.

Mike can be seen on the Mike Moore Ministries YouTube channel, his *How to Win* podcast, *Answers That Work with Mike Moore* show, and at conferences. He is the author of numerous, insightful books, including *Weep Not: Overcoming Grief, Disappointment, and Loss*, *The God of Abundance*, *Muted Voice*, and his latest release, *Help! My Mind Is Under Attack*.

He is married to his best friend and the love of his life, Kennetha. They have two adult children, Pastor Michael K. Moore and Tiffany Moore, daughter-in-law Michelle, and three beautiful granddaughters.

ABOUT MIKE MOORE MINISTRIES

Mike Moore Ministries, founded by Mike Moore, is a global ministry built on the powerful truth that "The Word of God Is the Answer" to every challenge in life. Through various materials, including books, and innovative media such as online content, social media, and digital platforms—Moore teaches that God's plan for His people goes beyond financial prosperity. It encompasses spiritual growth, physical health, strong relationships, mental well-being, and financial independence.

For more information and resources, visit **mikemoore.com** or call toll-free at 1-866-930-WORD (9673). And follow us on social media **@mikemooreministries**.

RESOURCES

Living with the ramifications of how mental health challenges can impact our lives can be overwhelming and self-defeating. Stress, anxiety, and depression can take over our well-being and leave us lost in a sea of suffering. We weren't intended to live this way or be separated from the fullness of life promised by God's love in His Word.

In *Help! My Mind Is Under Attack: Replace Inner Chaos with Enduring Peace*, Mike Moore provides insight on how we can change the way we face and overcome the origins of attacks on our minds. It's a call for us to live emotionally free of these burdens with a new peaceful life promised to us. You can break free and have victory!

Available in Paperback, E-Book, and Audiobook. Visit our shop at **www.mikemoore.com** to make a purchase. If you are interested in purchasing this or other Mike Moore Ministries' books in bulk, please email us at mmm@mikemoore.com or call toll free at 1-866-930-9673.

www.ingramcontent.com/pod-product-compliance
Lightning Source LLC
Chambersburg PA
CBHW041309240426
43661CB00045B/1497/J